PENGUIN SPECIALS

Penguin Specials fill a gap. Written by some of today's most exciting and insightful writers, they are short enough to be read in a single sitting — when you're stuck on a train; in your lunch hour; between dinner and bedtime. Specials can provide a thought-provoking opinion, a primer to bring you up to date, or a striking piece of fiction. They are concise, original and affordable.

To browse digital and print Penguin Specials titles, please refer to **penguin.com.au/penguinspecials**

LOWY INSTITUTE

The Lowy Institute is an independent, nonpartisan international policy think tank. The Institute provides high-quality research and distinctive perspectives on the issues and trends shaping Australia's role in the world. The Lowy Institute Papers are peer-reviewed essays and research papers on key international issues affecting Australia and the world.

For a discussion on *Rise of the Extreme Right* with Lydia Khalil and leading commentators on right-wing extremism, visit the Lowy Institute's daily commentary and analysis site, *The Interpreter*: **lowyinstitute.org/the-interpreter/debate/rise-of-the-extreme-right**.

Lydia Khalil is a Research Fellow at the Lowy
Institute and an Associate Research Fellow at
Deakin University. She began her counter-terrorism
and national security career after the September 11
attacks. She is a recognised expert on terrorism and
extremism, having worked for the White House
Office of Homeland Security, US Department of
Defense, the New York Police Department, Boston
Police Department and the Council on Foreign
Relations. She is a frequent media commentator
and has been widely published.

LOWY INSTITUTE

Rise of the Extreme Right

A LOWY INSTITUTE PAPER

LYDIA KHALIL

PENGUIN BOOKS

UK | USA | Canada | Ireland | Australia
India | New Zealand | South Africa | China

Penguin Books is part of the Penguin Random House group of companies
whose addresses can be found at global.penguinrandomhouse.com.

Penguin
Random House
Australia

First published by Penguin Books, 2022

Cover image by Warren Wong/Unsplash
Typeset by Midland Typesetters, Australia

Printed and bound in Australia by Griffin Press, an accredited
ISO AS/NZS 14001 Environmental Management Systems printer

A catalogue record for this
book is available from the
National Library of Australia

ISBN 978 1 76104 635 3

penguin.com.au

CONTENTS

CHAPTER ONE

A threat ignored

On a February morning in 2010, a single-engine Piper Cherokee light aircraft was on the runway at Georgetown Municipal Airport in Austin, Texas.

'Georgetown tower, Dakota 2889 Delta's ready for departure,' the pilot radioed the airport tower.

'89 Delta clear for take-off.'

'Thanks for your help. Have a great day,' the pilot responded.[1]

A mere ten minutes later, the pilot of the Piper crashed into the first and second floors of Echelon Building I, which housed an office of America's federal tax agency, the Internal Revenue Service (IRS). The crash killed the pilot and one victim. Thirteen more were injured.

As emergency management and police rushed to the scene and news reporters arrived to file stories, one question was on everyone's minds: what if this wasn't an accident? Any plane crash, especially into a building, automatically brought with it the spectre of the September 11 attacks of 2001.

As the day wore on, details began to emerge. The plane crash was no accident. But neither was it the work of an al-Qaeda affiliate.

The pilot was Joseph Stack, a white 53-year-old software engineer cum local musician. A day before slamming his plane into the exact floors that housed the IRS offices, he had driven his wife and step-daughter out of their family home and set it on fire.

Stack had a long history as an anti-tax protester and had stoushed with the IRS on multiple occasions in the preceding decades. At the time of the incident, Stack was being audited by the IRS for failure to report income.

Was the attack a desperate last gasp in Stack's personal vendetta against the IRS? Was it a part of his stubborn campaign to withhold income from the federal government? Was it the result of mental illness?

Stack had left behind a suicide note, what we might now call a manifesto – the all too familiar hallmark of the terrorist lone attacker. The manifesto was an indictment of corrupt corporations, the Catholic Church and government writ large, but particularly the IRS.

It made clear that this attack was not just the culmination of decades of personal grievances against the IRS, an organisation that he believed had uniquely targeted and tormented him.[2] He also linked his grievances to an anti-government, anti-tax movement. He was ideologically opposed to the federal government collecting taxes and wanted his attack to inspire others to take action against the government. Stack's suicide attack was the final act of his long history of anti-tax activism.

According to criminologist and Director of the Center for the Study of Hate and Extremism, Brian Levin, 'This was someone who wanted to declare war on the IRS and to have a movement continue after he was gone ... He wanted to light the fuse that would cause a general uprising by others who feel cheated by the tax system to act out violently.'[3]

Stack wrote in his manifesto:

I can only hope that the numbers quickly get too big to be white washed and ignored that the American zombies wake up and revolt; it will take nothing less. I would only hope that by striking a nerve that stimulates the inevitable double standard, knee-jerk government reaction that results in more stupid draconian restrictions people wake up and begin to see the pompous political thugs and their mindless minions for what they are. Sadly, though I spent my entire life trying to believe it wasn't so, but violence not only is the answer, it is the only answer.[4]

In the early 1980s, Stack was living in Southern California, at the time a 'hot bed of the anti-tax movement which was interlaced with pseudo legal, pseudo historical, conspiratorial ideas'.[5] As a form of protest, Stack and his former wife formed a 'home church', claiming tax exempt status. The US government declared it an illegal tax shelter, a ruling that Stack spent his time doggedly challenging.

Joseph Stack's suicide attack was a textbook act of terrorism. It was a very public assault, clearly meant to terrorise, indiscriminately harming civilians while also deliberately targeting government infrastructure in pursuit of political aims.

Yet media coverage of the attack glossed over Stack's history and ideological motivations. A CNN reporter intoned to the camera, 'There were fears that this was an act of terrorism. But it wasn't. It was simply one man's grudge against the IRS.'[6] *The New York Times* described Stack as 'generally easy-going, a talented amateur musician with marital troubles and a maddening grudge against the tax authorities'.[7]

Public officials also stubbornly avoided the 't' word. Austin police chief Art Acevedo instead called it the 'cowardly, criminal act' of a lone individual. The Department of Homeland Security assured that there was no 'nexus to terrorist activity'.[8]

The reluctance to categorise Stack as a terrorist was curious. Even as the September 11 attacks continued to occupy an outsized space in the American psyche and remained the driving force behind its national security policy, politicians, law enforcement and the media refused to use the label 'terrorist' for a man crashing a plane into a government building after writing an anti-government manifesto hoping for a 'big body count' that would cause a 'revolt'.[9]

At the time of Stack's attack, I had just finished a stint as a counter-terrorism adviser to the New York Police Department. I was disturbed by the dismissive reaction.

After years monitoring global terrorist activity, working with detectives on foreign and domestic investigations and living a street away from the excavated rubble that was the World Trade Center, it was incredibly disconcerting to see what I thought was a clear act of terrorism being labelled as the act of an individual in crisis just because it did not look like what we were conditioned to think of as terrorism.

The September 11 attacks were the first significant experience of terrorism for many, and they wedded an association of terrorism to jihadism, the terrorism associated with militant Islamist movements. Joseph Stack was a white, middle-class 'everyman'. He did not fit the popular image of a terrorist.

Preoccupation with jihadism allowed many to conveniently forget that before September 11, the most deadly terrorist attack committed in the United States was by Timothy McVeigh, another anti-government extremist, who in 1995 bombed the Alfred P. Murrah Federal Building in Oklahoma City, killing 168 people, including 19 children, and injuring more than 680. McVeigh was also a white, middle-class 'everyman' connected to the anti-government extremist movement. The spectacular nature of the September 11 attacks obscured the persistent threat of anti-government extremism in the United States.

On one hand, I understood the difficulties in investigating the incident as a terrorist attack. Despite the Patriot Act's expansion of terrorism offences, there remains no specific law in the United States that allows federal prosecutors to charge someone with 'domestic terrorism'. It was tempting to dismiss Stack's attack as a result of personal pathologies instead of an ideologically motivated act of violence. He did act alone, and he was motivated by personal animus that bled through into his political beliefs.

Homeland Security Secretary Janet Napolitano,

who also happened to have been one of the lead investigators for the McVeigh trial,[10] said at the time: 'He had his own personal issues and personal motives . . . He used a terrorist tactic, but an individual who uses a terrorist tactic doesn't necessarily mean they are part of an organized group attempting an attack on the United States.'[11]

And yet, just because someone acts alone does not mean they cannot be a terrorist. In fact, lone actor terrorism was on the rise. The September 11 attacks unleashed a massive military, bureaucratic and law enforcement effort aimed at stopping another highly coordinated international terrorist attack. As a result, those motivated to commit terrorism had to resort to working alone or in small cells. By 2010, the vast majority of terrorism was committed by individuals or informal cells, not centrally organised groups. They were motivated by a complex mix of personal grievances and ideological beliefs and were connected to broader movements, not through organisational membership or operational directives but through ideological affinity.

In my law enforcement work, I was privy to field reports and analysis showing a sharp and steady uptick in right-wing, anti-government attacks against law enforcement and government infrastructure. A great many who committed violence were lone actors or operated in small cells. An analysis of lone actor terrorism that occurred before and around the Austin plane attack found that '86% of the lone perpetrators belong to one or another right-wing extremist movement'.[12]

Yet, at the time, few understood that Joseph Stack's attack fitted into a growing tide of anti-government sentiment with a potential for violence, and that it should have been seen as an integral part of a broader right-wing extremist movement.

One of the few who did was historian and analyst Mark Pitcavage, a veritable walking encyclopaedia of extremist movements in the United States. For 25 years, Pitcavage had been tracking domestic US extremist movements through his work for the State and Local Anti-Terrorism Training Program, a Department of Justice initiative created after the Oklahoma City bombing to train law enforcement officers on domestic terrorism issues.

Pitcavage followed the anti-tax protest movement and the Stack case closely. I contacted him to ask what he made of it then and now. At the time, Pitcavage considered Stack's attack a borderline case, but ultimately landed on counting it on his list of right-wing terrorist incidents.

'The key thing for any act of terrorism is whether and to what degree it was motivated by ideology versus personal animus . . . The bottom line for us was his past history with the anti-tax extremist movement.' Pitcavage also remarked that 'Stack's actions fit into accepted definitions of terrorism – a pre-planned act or attempted act of significant violence by one or more non-state actors to further an ideological, social or political cause or to harm perceived opponents of such causes.'

I asked Pitcavage if he thought the anti-tax movement that motivated Stack was on the right-wing extremist spectrum. Before I could even finish asking the question, he interjected with an emphatic, 'Absolutely. The tax protest movement,' Pitcavage explained, 'is extremely important in the history of right-wing extremism because it essentially gives birth to the area of anti-government right-wing extremism known as the Patriot movement.'

The anti-tax movement, the sovereign citizen movement and the militia movement are what Pitcavage calls 'sister movements' that collectively make up the Patriot movement, which in turn forms the anti-government wing of right-wing extremism. It sits alongside, and sometimes overlaps with, the other lodestar of the extreme right: white supremacism.

Indeed, after Stack's attack, white supremacist groups hailed him as a hero. It didn't matter that he wasn't known to espouse white supremacist views. Users on Stormfront, the largest white supremacist internet forum in the world, posted at the time:

> 'This is just the beginning. Prepare for battle!'
> 'This was quite heroic. There is a gradual awakening underway. I wonder how racially conscious he was.'
> 'Things are heating up in America . . . This man won't be the last to do something like this.'[13]

The claiming of Stack by white supremacists seems like a quirk until you understand how the anti-government, anti-tax movement has always intersected with other elements of right-wing extremism. Dismissing Stack as mentally ill or only motivated by personal grievances meant that officials also dismissed the fact that right-wing extremist movements were alive and well in America.

The debate over Stack also reflected how much more limited our understanding of radicalisation to violence was at the time. But through advances in research on the psychological process of radicalisation to violence, we now understand a lot more. Far from disqualifying him from the terrorist label, Joseph Stack's personal grievances paved his path to radicalisation – they helped get him to the place where he decided violence was the only answer.

But if it is clearer in hindsight that Joseph Stack was a violent extremist, questions still remain. How should we understand his anti-government attack? Were there broader forces at play than mere definitional debates that allowed so many to dismiss Stack as a disturbed individual rather than part of a growing threat to the United States?

Few besides Pitcavage and fellow specialists understood the breadth of right-wing extremism and how its various movements intersected, or had the historical perspective to properly situate a terrorist attack by an anti-tax protester within the broader right-wing extremist milieu.

A few elected leaders called it out. Republican Congressional Representative Michael McCaul, whose representative district included Austin, Texas and who was then the ranking Republican on the House Committee on Homeland Security, put it succinctly: 'When you fly an airplane into a federal building to kill people, that's how you define terrorism.'[14] His Democratic colleague from Texas agreed. Unlike Napolitano, Representative Lloyd Doggett *did* compare the attack on the Austin IRS building to the Oklahoma City bombing.

But despite previous warnings by the Federal Bureau of Investigation (FBI) about the increasing number of anti-government domestic extremists, the Bureau ultimately decided that it would not treat this as a terrorist attack but was investigating the incident 'as a criminal matter of an assault on a federal officer'.

The reluctance to label the Austin suicide attack as terrorism was not the only instance of dismissing and politicising the brewing right-wing extremism threat around that time. A few months prior, the Department of Homeland Security (DHS) had released a memo assessing that:

> Rightwing extremists may be gaining new recruits by playing on their fears about several emergent issues. The economic downturn and the election of the first African American president present unique drivers for rightwing radicalization and recruitment.

It went on:

> . . . and the return of military veterans facing significant challenges reintegrating into their communities could lead to the potential emergence of terrorist groups or lone wolf extremists capable of carrying out violent attacks . . . DHS/I&A [Intelligence & Analysis] is concerned that rightwing extremists will attempt to recruit and radicalize returning veterans in order to boost their violent capabilities.[15]

The report was labelled FOUO – for official use only – and was meant for law enforcement consumption. But it soon found its way into the hands of the media and far-right politicians.

It was excoriated by many Republican politicians aligned with the Tea Party movement. Stack's attack came at the height of this movement – a populist conservative, anti-deficit, anti-tax group highly critical of the Obama administration that emerged after the 2008 Global Financial Crisis. As befitting its name – a reference to the 1773 Boston Tea Party where colonialists protested British tyranny and taxation by throwing chests of tea into Boston Harbor – a central plank of the Tea Party movement was a repeal of the tax code. The 'Tea' in Tea Party also stood for 'Taxed Enough Already'. Tea Party Republicans accused the Obama administration of painting US veterans as extremists, and conservative voters unhappy with the administration's policies as potential domestic terrorists. Far-right radio shock jock Rush Limbaugh told his listeners, 'This Department of Homeland Security report is nothing more than a partisan hit job filled with lies and innuendo that portrays any conservatism as right-wing extremism.'[16]

A number of Republican lawmakers called for DHS Secretary Janet Napolitano's resignation.

Republican Representative Michele Bachmann said, 'To me, it looks like the extremists are those running the DHS.'[17]

Napolitano ultimately bowed to political pressure, issued a public apology to veterans[18] and announced that the DHS was retracting the memo. The author of the memo, Daryl Johnson, who Republican opponents might have been surprised to learn was a registered Republican and once said, 'I personify conservatism', was run out of the Department.[19] The analytic unit he ran was disbanded and by 2010 there were no intelligence analysts at DHS working on domestic terrorism threats.[20]

This was despite many independent non-government organisations and researchers sounding the alarm about right-wing extremism and anti-government sentiment. According to a report written in 2009 (the same year as the rescinded DHS memo) by the Southern Poverty Law Centre, a non-government organisation (NGO) well known for tracking hate crimes and domestic extremism in the United States, 'almost a decade after largely disappearing from public view, right-wing militias, ideologically driven tax defiers and sovereign citizens are appearing in large numbers around the country . . . This is the most significant growth we've seen in 10 to 12 years.'[21]

Astonishingly, some elected Republicans went beyond hurling accusations at DHS and actually justified Stack's attack and the ideological motivations behind it. In February 2010, newly elected Republican Senator Scott Brown, who won an upset victory in the Democratic stronghold of Massachusetts on the back of the Tea Party movement, used the incident as a political talking point. 'I can just sense, not only in my election and certainly since being here in Washington, people are frustrated. They want transparency. They want their public officials to be accountable . . . Certainly no one likes paying taxes.'[22]

Then Iowa Republican and Congressional Representative Steven King, a man who has been labelled 'the US congressman most openly affiliated with white nationalism' and who would pave the way for Donald Trump by staking out similarly incendiary positions on race, immigration and dismantling government,[23] went even further. 'I think if we had abolished the IRS back when I first advocated then he wouldn't have had a target for his airplane.'[24] King went on to call for a fundraising effort for anti-tax protesters and urged his constituents to 'implode' their local IRS offices.[25]

Though it lives on in the lore of anti-government extremism, aside from a handful of terrorism experts and the immediate victims, the Austin suicide attack has been largely forgotten. The broader warning of the 2009 DHS memo, however, has come to pass.

Data collected by the Washington, DC-based Center for Strategic and International Studies in 2021 shows a surge in right-wing extremist-motivated incidents in the United States not seen for a quarter of a century, dwarfing all other ideologically motivated attacks from left-wing extremists and jihadists.[26] More recent DHS assessments found white supremacists will remain the most persistent and lethal extremist threat to the country.[27] The joint FBI–DHS Strategic Intelligence Assessment and Data on Domestic Terrorism released in May 2021 also found that right-wing extremists – particularly white supremacists, sovereign citizens and anti-government militias – 'remained a persistent source of violence'.[28]

While his administration made some attempts to address right-wing extremism, President Trump became an inspiration and galvanising force for right-wing extremists in the United States and around the world. After his election, there was a steady stream of right-wing extremist violence in the United States.

In August 2017, a massive rally called 'Unite the Right' occurred in Charlottesville, Virginia, organised ostensibly to protest the removal of a statue of Confederate General Robert E. Lee. In reality, it was a rally of white supremacists, neo-Nazis and far-right militias.[29] They banked on their presence attracting counter-protesters and came ready to scuffle with them and with police. Things turned deadly when a white supremacist rammed his car into a group of counter-protesters, killing Heather Heyer and injuring many others.[30]

When pressed to condemn the protesters, President Trump said there was violence on 'both sides' and that 'there were some very fine people' peacefully protesting the removal of the statue. His comments essentially applied a false moral equivalence to the white supremacists and counter-protesters.[31]

Another major incident occurred in 2018 with a mass shooting at the Tree of Life synagogue in Pittsburgh, where 11 were killed. It was the deadliest attack on Jews in American history and occurred within the context of rising hate crimes against Jews and racial minorities by right-wing extremists.[32]

With multiple mass shootings occurring only months apart, 2019 became a banner year for right-wing extremism. The deadliest was in Christchurch,

New Zealand, where Australian-born Brenton Tarrant gunned down 51 worshippers and injured scores more at two mosques as he live-streamed the attack.

New right-wing extremist threats also emerged. QAnon – a pro-Trump, fascist, anti-Semitic conspiracy movement arising out of an internet subculture – came to the fore during the Trump presidency and grew during the Covid-19 pandemic. Other far-right, anti-government movements were turbo-charged by the pandemic and intersected with conspiracy movements, leading to numerous plots, attacks and other acts of violence in protest against lockdown measures and government mandates. Right-wing extremists capitalised on the fear and uncertainty of the pandemic and the chafing against government intrusions in the name of public health.

It all reached a crescendo with the Capitol siege. With Trump having spent weeks undermining the validity of the 2020 presidential election result and ultimately refusing to peacefully cede power, pro-Trump and QAnon extremists mounted an insurrection to disrupt the Electoral College count and ratification on the Congressional floor. The audacity of the Capitol siege – the first time the Capitol building had been breached by an armed group since 1814, and incited by a sitting president, no less – came very close to upending the world's oldest continuous democracy.[33]

*

As alarming as this all is, the growing right-wing extremist threat is far from reliant on Trump, and its growth is not limited to the United States. It is a global issue. The United States has become a major exporter of right-wing ideology and narratives, and a recent US president is its key influencer. But the rise of the extreme right is connected to broader political and social factors, corresponding with the growth of far-right populism, disaffection with democracy, global capitalism and lack of trust in government and institutions around the world.

The United Nations Security Council Counter-Terrorism Committee has released multiple threat assessments outlining the increasing concern of member states about the growth and threat of right-wing extremism and terrorism around the world.[34] There has been upwards of a 320 per cent increase in right-wing extremism globally from 2016 to 2021.[35]

In Australia, intelligence and counter-terrorism officials have warned of the growing threat. In 2021, the Director-General of the Australian

Security Intelligence Organisation (ASIO) said right-wing extremist and white supremacist terrorism made up at least 50 per cent of the agency's caseload.[36] Also in 2021, Australia proscribed two right-wing extremist groups – The Base and Sonnenkrieg Division – as terrorist organisations; the first time the Australian government has ever listed right-wing extremist groups.

Recent investigative reports by the ABC, *The Age* and the anti-fascist White Rose Society detailed the extent of right-wing extremist activity in Australia, uncovering previously unknown connections between Australians and right-wing extremist movements, particularly in the United States.[37]

Far-right extremism is a significant and growing threat in Europe, too. In 2016, the number of extreme right-wing terrorist attacks increased by 43 per cent. A 2021 report published by the Center for Research on Extremism in Norway found a considerable rise in the number of right-wing extremist plots in Western Europe, particularly against Black minorities. Worryingly, many of them were committed by uniformed personnel. The RTV report contained a caveat that its dataset only included the 'most severe' incidents and that less severe attacks and plots were 'too many to be covered systematically and exhaustively'.[38]

The German Interior Minister declared right-wing extremism 'the greatest threat to security in our country' in 2021. Criminal activity and political violence associated with right-wing extremist groups are at their highest levels in Germany since recording began.[39] Right-wing extremist infiltration of the German Army became so concerning that Germany's Defence ministry had to disband an entire company of its Special Forces Command (KSK). As of 2020, there were 500 soldiers under investigation by military counter-intelligence for right-wing extremist sympathies.[40]

Growth is not limited to the Anglosphere or continental Europe. Right-wing extremism is also on the rise in Asia. In India, anti-Muslim violence, communal riots and mob attacks fuelled by the extremist Hindutva movement have grown.[41] In Prime Minister Narendra Modi, India has its own far-right populist leader with ties to extremist Hindu movements. Modi's rule has emboldened elements advancing an exclusivist Hindu nationalism that undermines India's longstanding multicultural identity.[42] Extreme ethno-nationalism and anti-Muslim sentiment have also rocked Sri Lanka and Myanmar, undermining pluralism and democracy.

Even these stark details don't reveal the full extent of the growth in right-wing extremism. They only indicate the number of terrorist attacks, foiled plots and arrests. They don't touch on the many hate crimes,[43] violent counter-protests, the increase in paramilitary group membership, vigilante violence and other interpersonal violence and crimes committed by extreme-right actors. They also don't touch on the observable growing acceptance of extreme right-wing ideas and narratives promoted by nominally non-violent groups and political parties within both established and emerging democracies.

And right-wing extremism is only predicted to increase.

CHAPTER TWO

What's in a name?

If the Austin suicide attack was a harbinger of a growing threat, it also reflected the increasingly urgent debate about what to call it.

I would like to think that today the Austin suicide attack would be more readily recognised as an act of terrorism. Yet there is still a debate about what *type* of terrorism.

After the Capitol siege, one of the Biden administration's first acts was to request a comprehensive review of domestic threats.[44] In that assessment, there is a string of references to threats and movements targeting racial minorities, immigrants, Jews and LGBTQI communities by fascists, neo-Nazis, white supremacists, violent conspiracy movements and various strands of the anti-government Patriot movement,[45] of which Stack was a part.

And yet the assessment does not call any of these threats 'right-wing extremism' when all would fall within that category.[46]

We are in a confounding situation. Countries and regions where right-wing extremism is on the rise – the United States, Australia, Canada and Asia – do not officially use the label 'right-wing extremism' even though that is how the threat is commonly understood by researchers, how it is referred to in the general discourse, and how it is described by transatlantic partners.

So why isn't that label used by these government agencies? As we will see, the reason goes beyond good faith debates about the definition. There is a concerted effort across many jurisdictions to erase the term 'right-wing extremism'.

*

But first it is important to acknowledge that the term 'right-wing extremism' *is* contested.[47] For that reason, it is important to clearly explain what experts mean when they use the term and make the case for why it should be used to describe various types of political and ideological extremism.

The term 'right-wing extremism' is used to refer to many different types of movements and actors – from fascists, white supremacists and neo-Nazis to anti-government extremists such as Joseph Stack, sovereign citizens, the Patriot movement and militias in the United States. It is also used to refer to groups ranging from European anti-Islam movements espousing Great Replacement conspiracies, to extreme exclusionary ethno-nationalists. As a United Nations report notes: 'It is not a coherent or easily defined movement, but rather a shifting, complex and overlapping milieu of individuals, groups and movements (online and offline) espousing different but related ideologies.'[48]

It can be confusing to use one term to reference multiple movements that, on the surface, appear unrelated. But they *are* connected in important and relevant ways and there is a strong case that we should consider them all a part of the same phenomenon. These shared characteristics encompass both the 'right' and the 'extreme' parts of the label.

First, why are all these movements and trends considered 'right'? When we say 'right wing', we are referring to a political and ideological orientation. The dyad of right/left to describe the political and ideological spectrum has its roots in the French Revolution.

In 1789, the French National Assembly formed to write a new constitution. The assembly was divided over how much power the King should have. Those who believed that the King should retain his veto power, as was tradition, sat to the right of the president of the assembly. Those who believed the King should not, and argued for a more fundamental transformation, sat to the left. Over time, the terms 'right' and 'left' shifted, but our understanding of 'right wing' as one who favours conservatism and tradition still stems from the French Revolution.

Italian political philosopher Norberto Bobbio argues that what distinguishes left and right is their attitude towards inequality.[49] According to Bobbio, the right believes that most inequality cannot be eradicated, that state interventions are largely incapable of reducing inequality, and that it should not be the state's responsibility to do so. Rather, right-wingers take the position that inequalities are inherent and inevitable,[50] and it is the individual's responsibility to overcome them should they wish.

For mainstream political parties, this generally manifests in policies that give greater weight to individual liberty over equality. To be right wing in an electoral democracy can mean to favour limited government intervention and reliance on market-based solutions. Those on the right also tend to believe in an inherent social or economic hierarchy, and they emphasise cultural, ethnic and national particularity.

The right-wing movements of today can be understood along a spectrum – from mainstream political movements and established conservative political parties, to the reactionary right, and the far right. The moderate or conservative right believe in limited government, tradition and minimal intervention in markets. The reactionary right opposes political and societal transformation. It is often nostalgic and advocates for the return of an imagined golden age. The far right is characterised by nativism and authoritarian tendencies. While it might work within a democracy or the electoral system to effect change, the far right does not believe in *liberal* democracy, refusing pluralism and minority protections.[51]

The extreme right is different because of its qualifier: *extreme*.

Extreme right-wing individuals and movements are extreme because they aim to change the fundamental nature of the system,[52] not work within it. They are revolutionary. Extremists reject conservatism. As one prominent right-wing extremist put it, 'conservatism is corporatism in disguise. I want no part of it.'[53]

Right-wing extremists reject democratic politics in favour of revolutionary violence. The extreme right justifies the use of violence as a means to effect the change they wish to see, and oppose the state's monopoly on the legitimate use of force.

Right-wing extremism is sometimes referred to as 'far right' or 'radical right' or 'extreme right'. These shades of right-wing belief are not static, nor are they separated by bold lines. Rather, the barriers can be blurry, which is part of what makes the risk of right-wing extremism so diffuse and difficult to combat, particularly in a democracy where elements of the extreme right bleed into far-right movements and the far right engages with the extreme right.

It's also important to note that right-wing extremist violence is a unique form of political violence, one with 'often fluid boundaries between hate crime and organised terrorism'. Because a lot of right-wing extremist violence manifests as hate crimes instead of mass casualty attacks targeting the general population, its scope can often be under-appreciated. Right-wing extremists also engage in what they call 'defensive' violence by taking part in rallies and protests where they know counter-protesters will be present and confrontation is likely, or they engage in purposeful confrontations with law enforcement.[54]

Scholars such as Cas Mudde and Elisabeth Carter argue that right-wing extremism is first and foremost anti-democratic. Carter's extensive review of different conceptualisations of right-wing extremism succinctly boils it down to 'anti-democratic opposition to equality',[55] with strands of the extreme right veering even more sharply from authoritarianism to fascism – a type of authoritarianism that puts a nation or race above the individual and supports forceful, often violent, suppression of any opposition.

Right-wing extremists view the current order as corrupt and on the brink of a conflict for which they must prepare. The predominant state is one of being under siege from a perceived enemy, whether it be communists or the Marxist left, woke cultural and political elites, immigrants, or inferior yet menacing races. Right-wing extremists advocate extreme measures to protect what they believe is under threat.

Right-wing extremism centres on exclusion – a conceptualisation or creation of 'the other' or the 'out group', considered a threat that thereby becomes a legitimate target of violence.[56] For right-wing extremists, the 'out group' usually includes immigrants, refugees, Black, Jewish and Muslim people or other traditionally marginalised groups, left-wing actors, governments and elites.[57] Right-wing extremists view their 'in group' as superior and their success as inseparable from the exclusion or destruction of others.[58]

The extreme right also has a long history and association with conspiratorial thinking.[59] Anti-Semitism forms the backbone of right-wing extremist conspiracy theories, but various anti-Communist, anti-Catholic, anti-globalist and anti-elite conspiracies feature prominently in right-wing extremist thinking. Recent research corroborates this conspiratorial tendency in modern right-wing extremist movements, finding that people with extreme right-wing views were more likely to engage in conspiratorial thinking and had paranoid ideations and a strong distrust of government.[60]

*

While researchers and experts have come to a working consensus on the concept of right-wing extremism, many governments around the world have not. Even though right-wing extremism has replaced jihadism as a first order threat in the West, and governments are now scrambling to address it, there is still a reluctance in some countries to name it.

The European Union and the United Kingdom use the term 'right-wing extremism'[61] in their policies and communications. But in Canada and the United States, and now in Australia, intelligence and security agencies no longer use the right-wing and left-wing labels to describe violent extremist movements.

Canada classifies violent extremist threats according to three broad categories: religiously motivated, ideologically motivated and politically motivated. The United States breaks down terrorism into foreign and domestic threats, but instead of the umbrella terms used by Canada, the United States breaks domestic violent extremism into seven categories. Threats that would fall under the spectrum of right-wing extremism are termed 'racially or ethnically motivated violent extremism' and 'anti-government/anti-authority violent extremism' in US government documents.[62]

Australia officially stopped using the term 'right-wing extremism' in early 2021. When ASIO Director-General of Security Mike Burgess delivered the agency's annual threat assessment in March 2021, he announced:

> From today, ASIO will be changing the language we use to talk about the violent threats we counter. We will now refer to two categories: religiously motivated violent extremism and ideologically motivated

violent extremism. Why are we making a change? Put simply, it's because the current labels are no longer fit for purpose; they no longer adequately describe the phenomena we're seeing . . . Our language needs to evolve to match the evolving threat environment.

I was baffled at the ASIO terminology change. Only months prior, ASIO testified to a parliamentary inquiry that 40 per cent of its caseload was related to right-wing extremism, and this number was growing.[63] Why suddenly make this terminology change? It didn't make sense.

If ASIO thought the term 'right-wing extremism' was not fit for purpose, then its new terminology certainly wasn't either; in fact it was even less so. The new terms were too vague and confusing, especially as the violent extremism landscape is more complex than ever. The terms flatten distinctions and lack the clarity needed to understand extremist movements.[64]

For one thing, *all* extremist movements are ideological. For example, Salafi jihadism, the ideology driving al-Qaeda and Islamic State, is not just religious, it also has a socio-political program.[65] Salafi jihadism is a system of political ideas – ergo, an ideology. To refer to jihadism as 'religiously motivated' is incredibly misleading. By separating ideology and religion in its definitions, ASIO is missing important connections between the two elements. It also ignores the fact that many variants of right-wing extremism are religiously motivated and appropriate extreme forms of Christian, Buddhist, Hindu, pagan, even satanic theologies.

This raises a question: if variants of right-wing extremism can intersect with religious beliefs, is jihadism also a form of right-wing extremism? While jihadism certainly has authoritarian, chauvinistic and supremacist characteristics, the difference is that it does not merely seek to move from democratic, liberal and pluralistic governance to illiberalism, authoritarianism or even fascism. Rather, jihadism is arguably even more revolutionary. It seeks to eradicate the nation-state system in its entirety and replace it with a global caliphate to govern the global *ummah*, or Muslim community. Not all forms of religious extremism are inherently right wing. But if religion is used in the service of an ideology that advocates for extreme ethno-nationalism, exclusivist identities, or to prop up a far-right or authoritarian government, it can and should be considered right wing.

I thought the erasure of the term 'right-wing extremism' so problematic, and the terminology change so misguided, that I approached ASIO directly to understand what was driving this decision.

I was under no illusions that my intervention would move the bureaucracy, but I thought it was important to register my objections as someone who has studied these movements, and perhaps more importantly as a former counter-terrorism practitioner who worked cases and devised counter-terrorism policies.

I asked for a meeting with the Director-General. Instead, I got a meeting with a mid-level spokesperson who went through talking points already made in public by the Director-General. I was allowed to view an unclassified memo outlining the new terms and categories. Supervised, of course. ASIO was living up to its reputation and literally reading over my shoulder.

I tried to engage in conversation with the ASIO rep, tried to ask questions about what was behind the shift and made the argument for why the terminology change was not particularly useful, how it made little conceptual sense and appeared to minimise the threat from right-wing extremism.

Unsurprisingly, the conversation didn't get very far. The spokesperson just repeated the talking points. I felt bad, honestly. When I was working in government, I would have been annoyed at being tasked with taking a meeting to justify the organisation's position to a researcher. It was all above their pay grade anyway.

To give ASIO the benefit of the doubt, the gamut of violent extremists is more complex and dynamic than ever. New movements tend to be more fluidly organised. Some defy simple categorisation. Many violent extremist plots are based on a hodgepodge of beliefs and grievances, often driven by disinformation and conspiracies.

ASIO said the new terms were the result of a lengthy consultation process with Australia's international counter-terrorism and intelligence partners. ASIO also argued that its terminology change was its attempt to address longstanding concerns of Muslim communities that using previous labels such as 'Islamic extremism' to describe jihadist extremists from al-Qaeda and Islamic State, for example, stigmatised Muslims[66] and associated an entire religion with extremism.[67]

But are the two terms ASIO is now using – religiously motivated and ideologically motivated violent extremism – an improvement? Do they help our security agencies better label, understand and address the threat environment? I don't think so, particularly regarding right-wing extremism.

When ASIO announced this change, other government agencies and some in the media stopped using 'right-wing extremism' and began to use ASIO's terminology.

In early 2021, there was a report that Australian police had arrested two men for possession of an improvised explosive device and extremist material. In a statement on the arrests, a South Australia Police spokesperson confirmed that police had conducted multiple raids across metropolitan Adelaide as part of an ongoing investigation, which ultimately led to arrests in relation to 'ideologically motivated violent extremism'.[68]

It wasn't until a leader of one of Australia's neo-Nazi groups confirmed that their members' homes had been raided that reporters were able to identify which group had posed enough of a threat to warrant investigation, raid and arrest. It was the National Socialist Network (NSN), a rebranded and expanded neo-Nazi group that emerged in Melbourne in late 2019. It now has supporters across Australia, having incorporated white supremacists from former groups including the Lads Society and Antipodean Resistance.

Up to this point, the NSN's members had engaged mostly in vandalism, assault and intimidation, such as putting up racist graffiti and a cross-burning in the Grampians National Park in Victoria.[69] But recent arrests, thwarted plots to use explosives, and the group's increased rhetoric justifying violence, demonstrate an escalation in the threat.

The reference from police that the arrests were related to 'ideologically motivated' violent extremism was curiously nondescript. It did a disservice to the public to hide behind these vague terms. It didn't adequately communicate that the public was facing an escalating threat from a growing neo-Nazi movement in Australia.

It was hard to escape the conclusion that the labelling change had to do with recent complaints made by those on the right side of politics. Prior to the announced terminology change, then Liberal Party Senator Concetta Fierravanti-Wells had grilled ASIO Director-General Mike Burgess multiple times over the issue.

Mirroring the interventions discussed earlier by right-wing politicians made in the United States, during a parliamentary committee hearing, the Senator complained to Burgess:

> I am concerned about . . . the use of the terminology of 'right'. 'Right' is associated with conservatism in this country, and there are many people of conservative background who take exception to being tarred with the same brush. I think that you do understand that your comments, particularly when you refer to them solely as 'right wing', have the potential to offend a lot of Australians.

Burgess replied:

I certainly understand your point, Senator. I totally
get it. My intention was not to offend any innocent
people in that regard. As I said before, it's unfortu-
nate that we refer to it as 'right-wing extremism',
but, in the absence of something else – maybe we
should look at a different label.

Senator Fierravanti-Wells went on to claim,
inaccurately, that, 'both fascism and socialism have
their antecedents in communism'. She chastised
Burgess, saying, 'I think the time has come, Director-
General, especially from you, to ensure that you
are very careful with the terminology that you use,
so that ordinary Australians, particularly those of
conservative background, are not offended.'

'I'm happy with that, Senator. I totally agree,'
Burgess replied.[70]

The exchange continued when Burgess next
fronted the committee. Senator Fierravanti-Wells:

I know that we've had an exchange about this and
we've also exchanged correspondence about it . . . If
I may say, with my almost 40 years of experience,
it is really important to get that labelling correct,
because what you don't want is a circumstance

where the labelling itself results in unwarranted and unnecessary angst and, as a consequence of that, reactions that could themselves be extreme. So I ask you to take that into account.

Burgess' response was, again, not to counter the inaccuracies or make the evidence-based case for the use of 'right-wing extremism'. Instead, he said, 'Thank you for raising it. We are reviewing the terminology we use, for this very reason . . .'

Senator Fierravanti-Wells is not the only right-wing politician to object. Various right-leaning politicians around the world take umbrage at the term 'right-wing extremism' and have made the same argument that by conjoining the terms 'right wing' and 'extremism' the implication is that people with conservative beliefs are extremists.

Under the Trump administration, US officials refused to use the term, making it difficult for the United States to coordinate with transatlantic partners to address a common threat. They argued that it would be giving extremists 'legitimacy' by placing them on the political spectrum. Or that some of the causes championed by right-wing extremists – such as the neo-Nazis advocating for the use of population control and violence to protect the environment – were not traditionally right wing.[71]

Right-leaning politicians might not like the association with right-wing extremists, but to that I might say, welcome to the world of the two-billion-strong Muslim community, who, since the September 11 attacks, had their entire religion stigmatised because of the violent extremists in their midst. Senator Fierravanti-Wells wasn't similarly exercised when ASIO wrote in its threat assessment that 'Sunni Islamic extremism remains ASIO's greatest concern.'[72]

Their objections also reflect a deep misunderstanding of how right-wing extremists view mainstream conservatives. In matter of fact, right-wing extremists are hostile to establishment conservative parties. As the Christchurch attacker succinctly put it in his manifesto, 'CONSERVATISM IS DEAD. THANK GOD.'[73]

Some far-right figures also try to draw a false equivalence between right-wing extremism and left-wing extremism. You can often observe far-right politicians and commentators playing up the threat from antifa (shorthand for 'anti-fascist' movements), blaming them for rioting and looting and calling for the movement to be labelled a terrorist organisation.[74] Right-wing extremists create fake antifa social media accounts calling for violence, spread false information that antifa actors are responsible for violence, and pose as left-wing extremists to fool law enforcement during protests and rallies.[75]

Left-wing extremists and the radical left are certainly part of the extremist landscape. From the 1960s to the 1980s, they were the largest violent extremist threat in the Western world. Like right-wing extremism, left-wing extremism can be illiberal. However, left-wing extremist violence has waned and, despite inflated concerns in some quarters about the threat from antifa, it currently poses a much lesser threat than right-wing extremism. The consensus among serious researchers and policymakers is that left-wing extremism is not a leading threat, and in its current form should be considered differently from other forms of violent extremism, in that its use and justification of violence is more incidental than structural.[76] Left-wing extremist activity can certainly increase polarisation, but experts in the sociology and tactics of antifa and the radical left classify their current activities as mostly 'non-violent'.[77]

Ironically, while muddying the proverbial waters with its terminology change, Australia's Director-General of ASIO said in his address, 'We are conscious that the names and labels we use are important. Words matter. They can be very powerful in how they frame an issue and how people think about it.' That is all too true.

Definitions and terminology might seem unimportant in the grand scheme of things, but there is power in naming. How authorities and societies identify, describe and define the world around us is incredibly consequential. They give us a common way to communicate. Naming and labelling help us break taboos, denote priorities, legitimise and repudiate, all of which are essential aspects of addressing violent extremists and the harm they can do to society.[78]

It is also precisely because of the sensitivity in right-leaning political circles that a delineation of right-wing extremism is necessary and why the qualifier 'extremism' is important. And while acknowledging that right-leaning politics is different from right-wing extremism, there can also be troublesome connections between the two that mainstream right parties and politicians need to acknowledge and address.[79]

Though it could be argued that extreme-right movements are too diverse to be lumped together under one umbrella term, there is an equally compelling case that they need to be understood together.[80] If we don't, we can miss the connections between dangerous movements.

If we keep referring to a movement as vaguely 'anti-government' or 'ideologically motivated', we can't understand what form that extremism takes. If we are too specific with our labels – for instance, referring to white supremacists or Hindu extremists as ethnically or racially based supremacists without also labelling them right-wing – we fail to see that supremacist beliefs are integral to right-wing extremism. If we refer to QAnon as a conspiracy-based extremist movement without also placing it within the right-wing extremist spectrum we miss identifying the connections between conspiracism, anti-Semitism and right-wing ideology. Identifying extreme anti-immigration movements such as Identitarianism – a pan-European far-right nationalist ideology originating in France – without attaching the label 'right-wing' means we forego the opportunity to understand how important anti-immigration stances are to the development of right-wing extremism.

While we don't want to simplify or over-determine the linkages between these movements, if we don't understand and label them as part of the right-wing extremism spectrum,[81] we miss seeing the through-lines.

CHAPTER THREE

Structural conditions and personal appeals

'Who knows what evil lurks in the hearts of men?'

This catchphrase introduced the pulp fiction figure The Shadow, aka Kent Allard, a First World War pilot, playboy and crime fighter. The Shadow was a character in the eponymous radio series created by Walter B. Gibson in the 1930s during the rise of fascism. While The Shadow, a precursor and prototype for subsequent superheroes – who may have their own fascist tendencies via a penchant for vigilante justice[82] – was able to answer this question, decades of research on violent extremism has not quite caught up to him.

There is no single process to radicalisation. There is no 'profile'. What we know about human behaviour and how it intersects with structural conditions and social movements is incomplete. Individuals involved in violent extremist movements come from a wide variety of backgrounds and circumstances. Stereotypes of who might be a right-wing extremist – white, male, racist, rural or suburban, with a self-styled militia image and a 'Make America Great Again' hat – might often be true, but just as often don't hold.[83]

While we might not be able to predict who exactly may become involved in violent extremism or know the precise concoction that motivates individuals to hatred and violence, there are broad trends driving the growth of right-wing extremism. Across the Anglosphere, in Europe, Asia and elsewhere, transnational trends are fuelling individual grievances and resentments that are funnelling people into right-wing extremist beliefs and movements.[84]

Right-wing extremist movements have been around for a long time and there is a large body of work examining their history. But there is something different about the growth of right-wing extremism over the past two decades. Multiple factors are colliding and colluding, resulting in a perfect storm that has brought about an unprecedented surge of right-wing extremism.

Considering some of the ideas espoused by right-wing extremists – such as Nazism, or conspiracies positing that global elites are actually lizard people trafficking children to drink their blood – it is sometimes hard to believe that these movements could gain appeal. So, what is driving more people to right-wing extremist sympathies?

There is no doubt that the world has undergone profound stress and upheaval in this century: environmental crisis, a global financial crisis, chasms of inequality, and now a global pandemic. In periods of social, political and economic uncertainty, extremism can grow, and the disaffected can be recruited into these movements.[85]

To demonstrate the complex structural dynamics at play in the growth of right-wing extremism, I'll discuss four factors: globalisation and global inequality, the exponential spread of disinformation and misinformation, the climate crisis, and global democratic decline.

GLOBALISATION AND GLOBAL INEQUALITY

Globalisation and the accompanying rise in inequality are key structural elements driving right-wing extremism.[86]

Since the 1980s, most countries have experienced rising inequalities in wealth.[87] Studies by French economist Thomas Piketty describe how this inequality is tied to political ideology, and how the political platforms of both right and left political parties have led to more global inequality.[88] It used to be that left-wing parties were more focused on advocating for workers' rights, the welfare state and income redistribution, while right-of-centre parties protected the interests of capital and the business elite. However, left-of-centre parties have now become less focused on the economic issues of the working and middle classes, instead concentrating on identity, culture and the other preoccupations of the educated elite, leaving no party meaningfully working towards economic redistribution.

There are caveats, of course, and no doubt many left-of-centre political actors would quibble with this characterisation. But Piketty's argument that mainstream democratic politics on both the left and right has become dominated by the elite is compelling. Modern mainstream politics in many democracies has become what he calls a 'multi elite' political system, where establishment left and right political parties have a broadly neoliberal, global outlook and reflect more the views and interests of those elites rather than the locally situated average middle- or working-class voter, who is left feeling abandoned and convinced that the political and economic system does not work for them.

The 2008 Global Financial Crisis underscored

the belief that not only are politics and institutions primarily responsive to the interests of elites, but that elite interests have created a catastrophe for the rest of us. The Great Depression triggered an era of political extremism in the 1930s[89] and data collected after the 2008 financial crisis found similarly that low economic growth in its aftermath was associated with more extremist preferences.[90]

Instead of growing pressure for a social democratic solution or expansive New Deal-type programs, we have instead seen a rise in xenophobic, nativist, populist, identity-based far-right politics, high rates of voter absenteeism and the growing appeal of extremist movements.[91] Social democratic societies such as those in Australia, Canada and the Scandinavian countries have better redistributive economic policies and social safety nets, but they have not been immune to growing extreme and far-right tendencies. Many citizens have either turned against democratic politics or are seeking solutions outside establishment politics and institutions.

Globally, since the 1980s, the share of income going to the top one per cent has risen sharply. A wealthy transnational global elite is sucking up global wealth, and mainstream national political parties on the right and left have been complicit. Neoliberalism, particularly in advanced economies, has failed to live up to its promise of providing economic stability and freedom. This has led many to reject global governance and free trade, and instead retreat to narrow nationalism.[92]

This phenomenon also feeds into extreme-right conspiracy theories about a corrupt global cabal that wants to create a 'New World Order' – a far-right conspiracy theory whose origins go back hundreds of years, but which really took off after the establishment of the United Nations. The New World Order conspiracy claims that a powerful but secret global elite aims to take over the world and establish a global dictatorship.[93] What was once the province of the crackpot fringe has now moved into the mainstream, with more and more people on the left and right believing in versions of a conspiracy theory 'that global elites are manipulating us and taking away our rights and conspiring to abrogate national sovereignty and establish the world state'.[94]

The post-1990s period of hyper-globalisation has also left many displaced. In multiple advanced economies, international economic integration has occurred alongside domestic disintegration, deepening the divide between winners (professional, educated, cosmopolitan, skilled) and losers (the less educated, those working in industries that cannot globalise).[95] This has inflamed anti-elite sentiment within democracies and triggered a turn towards authoritarianism and exclusionary nationalism by those who feel economically, socially or politically ostracised by globalisation. Far-right political parties and extremist movements have responded by stoking anti-elite sentiment and inflaming cultural and identity divisions for political gain.

However, even if we accept the link between extremism and economic factors, study after study has debunked the thesis that economic insecurity alone leads to extremism and terrorism.[96] Many people involved in right-wing extremism come from comfortable, stable and secure backgrounds. In fact, many far-right influencers and proponents are themselves from the elite.

It is not so much that economic inequality and precarity stemming from globalisation are driving the growth of the extreme right, but that these factors are contributing to insecurity and anxiety around *status* – particularly the status of ethnic, racial or national majorities that are used to being the 'winners' of the system. Their resentments about loss of status[97] are driving anti-establishment, anti-elite and anti-immigration attitudes. They are also driving the appeal of right-wing extremist narratives about the perceived causes of this loss of status, as well as right-wing extremist solutions.

The doyenne of terrorism studies, Martha Crenshaw, tells us that it is not the objective conditions of participants in extremist movements that matter most, but their perceptions of their circumstances, their grievances and sense of injustice.[98] Influencers and leaders of right-wing extremist movements exploit these anxieties and resentments and focus them towards a clear and concrete point of blame.

Thomas Sewell, a leader in Australia's neo-Nazi movement, approaches potential followers in this way. He says of the status anxiety of many white young men:

> They are going to see that they are never going to afford a home. If they do, it's going to be in the middle of nowhere. They are going to be spending two hours in traffic to get to work in some dead-end job [that they] had to go to university for four years [to get]. They are in all this debt. The whole thing is geared against them. Probably not until they get to 40 can they even afford a family, so they can't even breed. So can we continue white people existing in this country if we don't have the economics geared for us to breed?[99]

DISINFORMATION

For as long as there have been humans, there have been lies, innuendo, half-truths and deceptions. There is a theory among social psychologists that belief in conspiracy theories may even be an evolutionary mechanism.[100] But the digital age has allowed for the unprecedented spread of disinformation, misinformation and conspiracy theories.

Disinformation (false, inaccurate or misleading information designed, presented and promoted intentionally to cause harm) and misinformation (false or untrue information, unknowingly spread) are so rife that specialists had to come up with a new field of study – infodemiology – to understand their dynamics. The World Health Organization (WHO), which held its first infodemiology conference in the wake of the turbo-charged growth in misinformation and disinformation during the Covid-19 pandemic,[101] has defined it as 'too much information including false or misleading information in digital and physical environments', which contributes to confusion, disillusionment and risk-taking behaviour and undermines trust in authorities and institutions.[102] Spreading disinformation has become a form of attack in and of itself, with right-wing extremist groups encouraging followers to spread disinformation to exacerbate tensions and undermine government authority and social cohesion.[103]

J. M. Berger, a scholar of extremism and technology, argues that social media platforms shatter our 'consensus reality' – the idea that we know what is true and what is real through the confirmation of those around us, and that 'the more people who agree on a fact the more we understand it to be real'. Without consensus reality, we have no common factual basis, therefore we cannot have an exchange of ideas or debate and thus can't solve collective problems. This shattering of consensus reality, which has occurred largely as a result of our interactions online, has contributed to the growth of extremism via the hardening of views, the consolidation of exclusivist identities and an increasing susceptibility to conspiracy theories.[104]

Belief in conspiracy theories is heightened during times of complex transformation and crisis,[105] when people often feel powerless against the sweeping tides of change.[106] While conspiracy theories are often implausible, they offer unambiguous, linear, causal explanations of complex or uncertain events. They confer a sense of specialness to those who believe they have access to insider knowledge about the structures and forces that move our world[107] or who are, in the current parlance, 'red pilled' – a reference to the 1990s movie *The Matrix* in which the protagonist is offered either a red pill, which allows him to learn unsettling truths, or a blue pill, which leaves him in contented ignorance.

Recent research confirms that 'a conspiracy mentality leads to increased violent extremist intentions'.[108] The FBI has assessed that 'Anti-government, identity-based and fringe political conspiracy theories very likely will emerge, spread and evolve in the modern information marketplace over the near term . . . occasionally driving both groups and individuals to commit criminal or violent acts.'

The extreme right has a long association with conspiratorial thinking,[109] but the intersection between conspiracy theories and right-wing extremism is now most prominently encapsulated in the QAnon phenomenon.

Even by the standards of conspiracy theories, QAnon is pretty wild. The theory claims that every US president until Trump has been a puppet put in place by a global cabal of power brokers – the deep state – made up of Democrats, Hollywood elites, the Catholic Church, the international banking system, the mainstream media, the pharmaceutical industry and tech companies that are enriching themselves, controlling world events and perpetrating a child-murdering sex cult while keeping the rest of us ignorant and enslaved.

QAnon adherents believe there is a privileged government insider with 'Q level' access to classified intelligence who is leaking information – known as 'Q drops' – to the public about a secret plan to thwart the deep state. These cryptic Q drops – first posted on the anonymous online 8chan forum, then Reddit, and from there migrating and flourishing on mainstream social media platforms such as Facebook – are then deciphered by believers.

Q drops form #ThePlan, which explains how Trump is prosecuting his resistance to the deep state. The Plan started with Trump's election and will culminate with #TheStorm, a series of indictments and then public executions or imprisonment of members of the deep state. During the 2020 US presidential election, QAnon also pushed the 'Big Lie', the claim that the election results were tampered with and that Trump was the rightful winner. QAnon promoted the idea that the Capitol siege would be #TheStorm – the day of reckoning for the deep state.

QAnon first emerged in 2017, but grew exponentially during the Covid-19 pandemic and the Black Lives Matter movement. It metastasised so quickly because of the internet, but also because it opportunistically gobbled up other conspiracy theories and anxieties around Covid vaccinations, mass protests against racial injustice, and polarising elections. By acting as a type of 'ur-conspiracy',[110] it incorporated and accommodated numerous other conspiracy theories old and new, and opportunistically engaged current events into its conspiratorial narrative. In the process, it inspired plots, attacks and violations of government lockdown measures around the world, including in Australia. QAnon has radicalised people to target political leaders, public health facilities and minority communities they believe are responsible for the spread of the virus. It has also intersected with far-right movements.

Some experts have likened QAnon to a new and still evolving 'hyper religion' deeply intertwined with popular and political culture.[111] This is a useful way of understanding the practice and community of QAnon believers, but it is also important to remember that, at its core, QAnon is an anti-Semitic, anti-establishment, fascist conspiracy theory that dovetails with right-wing extremist beliefs and goals.

The core myth of QAnon is that a secret cabal is taking over the world by kidnapping children and drinking their blood to gain power, and that this cabal is comprised of individuals in high positions financed by Jewish money. This is a rehashing of the old 'blood libel' conspiracy theory outlined in *The Protocols of the Elders of Zion*, which animated Nazi Germany. In fact, it is a modern internet version of the same anti-Semitic conspiracies around ritual murder and harm of children that have existed since the twelfth century.

QAnon is not just a repackaging of anti-Jewish conspiracies, but a repackaging of Nazi symbols, terms and themes. QAnon symbols and motifs carry barely veiled references to fascist Germany. QAnon's slogan, 'The Coming Storm', which refers to the day of mass arrests of this cabal, echoes the 'Night of the Long Knives' purge of Nazi leaders by Adolf Hitler in 1934. QAnon t-shirts read, 'Camp Auschwitz: Work brings freedom', the slogan that greeted prisoners at Nazi concentration camps. Another Q slogan, '6MWE', stands for 'Six Million Wasn't Enough', a reference to the number of Jews killed in the Holocaust. GhostEzra, one of the biggest QAnon online influencers, was recently outed as a Florida evangelical pastor who has moved from QAnon's coded anti-Semitism to explicit Nazi propaganda and white supremacy.[112]

THE CLIMATE CRISIS
Given that many on the right have been sceptical of climate science and that right-wing political parties have been slow to enact legislation to blunt the

impacts of climate change, it might be surprising to learn that among some right-wing extremists, concern about the environment is a motivating factor. But 'Eco-fascism' has emerged as one response to the degradation of the environment.

Patrick Wood Crusius, who was inspired by the Christchurch attack and committed a copycat mass shooting in an El Paso Walmart that killed 20 people in 2019, revealed in his manifesto that, in addition to anti-immigrant sentiment, he was motivated by environmental concerns. His manifesto was pithily titled 'An Inconvenient Truth', a reference to Al Gore's famous documentary on climate change. Crusius wrote:

The decimation of the environment is creating a massive burden for future generations. Corporations are heading the destruction of our environment by shamelessly overharvesting resources. This has been a problem for decades . . . Everything I have seen and heard in my short life has led me to believe that the average American isn't willing to change their lifestyle, even if the changes only cause a slight inconvenience. The government is unwilling to tackle these issues beyond empty promises since they are owned by corporations. Corporations that also like immigration because more people means a bigger market for their products . . . So the next logical step is to decrease the number of people in America using resources. If we can get rid of enough people, then our way of life can become more sustainable.[113]

Crusius is parroting core eco-fascist ideas. Eco-fascism draws a link between the environmental effects of climate change and overpopulation and global migration. It posits that 'population cleansing' is the solution for the climate crisis. It reworks old Nazi ideas of the *völkisch* movement rooted in the notion of 'blood and soil', a belief that a racially defined people were organically connected to a particular land and that a return to agrarian life was a counterweight to a corrupt, polluting cosmopolitanism.[114] Eco-fascist ideas also motivated the Christchurch terrorist and movements such as the Atomwaffen Division.[115] This is a new generation that idealises Nazi Germany as a paragon of environmentalism.

The lack of effective coordinated action on climate change has opened space for the revival of fascist ideas that promote chauvinistic solutions to environmental concerns. Protecting the environment becomes not a global collective effort that will benefit humankind and the natural world, but a means to exclude or eradicate certain segments of the population for the benefit of those believed to be organically connected to a particular place.

Eco-fascists blame the 'capitalist class' and corporate elites for the degradation of the environment. They oppose industrialisation and globalisation and believe immigration and multiculturalism are threats to the natural world.[116] They mix their programs of agrarianism, natural health and alternative wellness with racism. Eco-fascism has also become a vehicle to promote anti-Semitism, with Jews presented as a de-racinated, corrupt, cosmopolitan elite destroying the land through industrialisation, mass migration and global capitalism at the expense of 'real people'.

Fears among certain right-wing extremists about ecological disaster from climate change are intertwined with opposition to immigration. Posts from an Australian eco-fascist Facebook page are rife with memes advocating for a return to the White Australia policy and denigrating the Greens Party for claiming to be for the environment while also welcoming refugees.[117]

As the climate crisis grows, there is a temptation to find an easy enemy to blame – another race, another nation, another group of people. Right-wing extremists not only blame them for the climate crisis, but advocate targeted violence against them. As one

American extremist put it: 'These people have names and addresses. Their kids have names and addresses, and the capitalist class, by hook or by crook, has to be liquidated . . .'[118]

GLOBAL DEMOCRATIC DECLINE

Former US president Ronald Reagan famously said that 'the nine most terrifying words in the English language are "I'm from the government, and I'm here to help."'[119] Small government has been a stalwart position of mainstream right parties for decades. But some elements of the right have expanded from small government positions to espousing extreme libertarian, even anti-government, positions. Anti-establishment and anti-elite sentiment is rife and so too is the feeling that democratic governance is ineffective at best and corrupt at worst.[120]

Freedom House is a research institute that advocates for the support and development of democracies around the world. It was first established in New York in 1941 to counter isolationism and fascism, and promote American involvement in the Second World War. Through its signature *Freedom in the World* annual report, Freedom House tracks and measures developments in democracy and liberties around the globe. In the 1970s and 80s, it was focused on the promotion of democracy in the

Soviet sphere of influence and monitored threats to democracy during the Cold War. In the 1990s and early 2000s, it expanded its efforts to monitoring and promoting human rights in the Middle East, Latin America, Africa and Asia. In the second decade of the new millennium, it turned its attention inwards, towards the decline in democratic integrity in bulwarks such as the United States, Europe and Australia. Instead of promoting human rights, liberties and democratic governance in fragile emerging democracies, the worry now is that such norms are eroding in what political scientists call 'consolidated democracies'.

In recent years, Freedom House has published a steady stream of reports on democracy's decline and how it is under attack by right-wing populists who 'reject pluralism and demand unchecked power to advance the particular interests of their supporters, usually at the expense of minorities and other perceived foes'.[121] The title of its latest report is *Democracy under Siege*. It outlines the myriad ways that 'the long democratic recession is deepening'.[122] Recording the fifteenth consecutive year of democratic decline, the report describes how this is affecting longstanding democracies such as the United States and India, where right-wing populist leaders have emerged.[123]

The Economist Intelligence Unit's Democracy Index also saw more countries move from 'full democracies' to 'flawed democracies' in 2020. The International Institute for Democracy and Electoral Assistance, an intergovernmental organisation committed to the rule of law, human rights and the basic principles of democracy, has reported that backsliding democracies have doubled in the past decade.[124] For the first time, it added the United States to its list, citing Trump's stoking of the stolen election theory, his failure to concede to the peaceful transfer of power, restrictive voting rights legislation, and growing polarisation.[125]

While there has been a rise in democratic participation and political awareness in the past few years and in some instances record voter turnout, there has concurrently been greater polarisation, eroding social cohesion and lack of trust in government institutions in many democracies.[126] Measurements around the effectiveness of government to provide solutions to people's problems in democracies have shown a sharp drop.[127] Political accountability and competitiveness in democracies are declining, with many people feeling like the system is rigged. Instead, there is a perception that politicians are only responsive to special interests, are puppets of corporate masters, or are only in public service for personal gain. They are not responsive to the needs of those they govern, or do not include them in decision making. This perception of 'unrepresentative' democracy has led to declining levels of trust. In Australia, thanks to democracy sausages, compulsory voting laws and widespread perception (if not reality[128]) of egalitarianism, democratic health is strong by many measures, yet levels of trust in government in Australia are among the lowest in the world.[129]

Democratic decline has provided opportunities for anti-democratic forces to capture the disaffected and disenfranchised. As a result, we see a growth in the appeal of the 'strong man' model of governance – a 'get things done' type of leadership that also tends to embrace nativism, intolerance and disregard for democratic processes and institutions. A wave of far-right populist leaders has been elected in democracies around the world: Trump in the United States, Jair Bolsonaro in Brazil, Viktor Orbán in Hungary, Rodrigo Duterte in the Philippines, and Narendra Modi in India. France's Marine Le Pen also attracts growing support.[130]

The political appeal of far-right politicians has emboldened the extreme right. They find legitimacy in leaders who echo their talking points and who are willing to scuttle liberalism and egalitarianism. Yet for extremists, these leaders don't go far enough, convincing extreme-right actors that their ideological goals have to be pursued by violence.

While political, economic, historical and social factors are clearly driving the growth of the extreme right, they are not sufficient to explain what draws people into right-wing extremism. After all, billions of us live under similar conditions. Aren't we all experiencing global democratic decline, growing inequality and environmental degradation? Yet clearly not all of us are flocking to these movements. There has to be some sort of personal appeal or cognitive disposition at work in addition to these structural conditions.

What makes some people immune and others responsive to extremist appeals that opportunistically capitalise on these conditions? 'What evil lurks in the hearts of men?'

Jeff Schoep is one man who has had a very public change of heart. For more than two decades, Schoep was the leader of America's largest neo-Nazi organisation, the National Socialist Movement (NSM). He organised anti-immigration and white supremacist rallies alongside the Ku Klux Klan and other white supremacist and neo-Nazi organisations. He was a prolific recruiter, particularly of teenagers.[131] Schoep was involved in myriad violent confrontations with counter-protesters over the years and is named in a civil lawsuit against the organisers of the 2017 Unite the Right rally in Charlottesville.[132]

In 2019, Schoep became one of the highest profile extremists to publicly disavow white supremacy. During his waning days in the movement, he participated in the documentary *White Right: Meeting the Enemy* by Deeyah Khan, a Norwegian journalist of Pakistani descent.[133] This experience, and the relationship he developed with Ms Khan, is what Schoep credits for prompting him to disengage with the movement.

There is scepticism in some quarters about his sincerity and the motivations behind Schoep's disavowal of white supremacy. Some say it is a way for him to evade accountability and to create a new career and persona as a 'former' – the term used for ex-extremists who then go on to do intervention work to disengage others from extremist movements – without truly reckoning with his culpability.[134]

Schoep insists his disavowal is genuine and says he is committed to undoing the harm he caused by working to pull others away from extremism. I connected with him after listening to him speak at a roundtable on de-radicalisation.

There was no way I could determine his sincerity or his true motivations, but I did want to understand what was personally appealing about white supremacy for him, why he was involved in the movement for so long and how he first connected with extremist ideas. Unlike many current or former extremists, he was willing to talk.

Countering the stereotype that people become radicalised because of a troubled upbringing, Schoep says he came from a 'decent family' who didn't approve of his neo-Nazi sympathies and tried to dissuade him from his involvement in the NSM.

Nor did he think that he was doing anything wrong or evil. Schoep told me:

> Most people don't want to be the bad guy . . . I sure didn't. I didn't see myself that way. Members of extremist movements don't see [their involvement] as bad or evil . . . While hate is a big part of white supremacy, it is not the factor that first gets people involved in these types of things . . . A lot of times it's grievances or trying to find a sense of belonging; some people are there searching for something, it could be anything.[135]

I asked Schoep what first drew him into the movement if it wasn't the hateful ideas and rhetoric he ended up spewing. What was he searching for that he found in white supremacy and neo-Nazism?

For Schoep, it started as a way of reconnecting with his family's history. His grandfather, while not a card-carrying member of the Nazi Party, was conscripted into Hitler's army in the Second World War. It wasn't often discussed in his family; his grandmother discouraged him from asking about it too much. Still curious, he would approach his grandfather during quiet moments where he would draw out stories about his experiences. In these conversations, he found a point of connection with his grandfather and his family's history.

Schoep also grew up with battle-scarred stories from his great uncles who fought in the war, and his grandmother's experience living in and being deported from Prussia after the war. 'It made me very angry to hear about these stories [of displaced Germans],' Schoep said.

Schoep's interest in his family's history and German history more broadly compelled him to delve deeper into Second World War history and eventually Nazi ideology. I got the sense from Schoep that his family's reluctance to openly discuss their history also gave it the appeal of the forbidden. There was a certain adventure in mining this special, exotic and hidden place where his family history and his own identity lay.

A trip to Germany as a teenager led him to seek out neo-Nazis directly, believing they were a continuation of Hitler's movement, the movement his family fought for and that was part of his heritage. 'I was hoping to come across them, I thought it would be cool or interesting to make that connection.'[136] He wasn't successful. Though he did come across some neo-Nazis during an outing with a German cousin, his broken German gave him away as an American. It was the 1980s and most neo-Nazis of the time weren't too keen on Americans.

When he returned from Germany, he began to clash more with his family. He says he became disruptive and disobedient, which led him to being thrown out of home at 16. Away from his family's rules, living with a girlfriend, he continued to seek out information on Nazism, including reading *Mein Kampf*. He was still eager to connect to the broader movement.

'I didn't find an actual organisation [to join] until I was 18 and I found it in a library book of all places.'

In the back of a sociology book in the local library, he found a list of all the white supremacist organisations operating in the United States at the time.

He wrote to all of them. One of them, Christian Identity, was coming to the Minnesota State Fair, near where he was living, and it was there that they connected him to other white supremacist and Patriot movement folks. He eventually joined the NSM.

Schoep insists that the radicalisation and the hate came later, only after he joined the movement. 'I wasn't raised to hate people or anything like that. It wasn't my motivation for joining. I felt like I was going to save my race, save my people, save my country. That was my narrative.'[137]

This altruistic narrative might seem self-serving, but it can be part of the psychological process of radicalisation. Termed 'parochial altruism',[138] it is the concept of sacrifice for a group or acting against one's own benefit to protect an 'in group'. In Schoep's case, his group was white people.

'You start off thinking you are doing something good, but all of a sudden you start hating people. You start de-humanising the so-called 'other' – the Jews, the Blacks, the immigrants, the Muslims. In that process, you as an individual start to lose touch with your own humanity.'[139]

The environment also becomes very closed off and cult like. 'It's an echo chamber. You are in this bubble and behind these barriers,' Schoep says of the white supremacist movement.

I asked Schoep about his time organising demonstrations with the Klan, facing off against counter-protesters and the violence that ensued. What did those confrontations do for him? He said that, as leader, he actively sought out these experiences, that manufacturing and confronting an enemy was good for the movement's development and morale.

'One time, we organised a rally with the Klan in Mississippi and there were no counter-protesters, and as far as morale goes, it was the worst . . . because we're not fighting and not having people yelling or confronting us. It was a defeat in a sense. Usually afterwards you have an after-party, but not this time.' This time, the Klan packed up their robes. There was no rush, no sense of accomplishment or subversion.

He contrasted that experience with an earlier rally he held in New Jersey where confrontation with counter-protesters led to street fighting. Even reflecting on events years later, Schoep was animated and energised: 'Police are getting called; I knocked a guy out with [a] chair. But even though people got really hurt, it was a big morale boost. We saw ourselves as the vanguard of the white race. We were the defenders on the frontlines.'

The appeal of danger and heroics was coupled with a protective sense of community.

In a lot of ways, I felt safe because I had an army behind me. I could snap my fingers at any time and have people at my house with guns in a minute, you know? So, in that sense, I felt very safe.

At the same time, you have enemies and there was a constant fear . . . I experienced law enforcement raids on my house three times . . . my kids to this day are traumatised by that experience of doors being kicked in and guns drawn . . . You also have all the infighting [within the movement] . . . We had people who died, took their own lives. A really close friend of mine was shot to death in his sleep. More death and destruction than you can imagine . . . and we would justify these things by saying they died for the cause.

Like extremists of all stripes, Schoep seemed unable to come to terms with life's complexities and contradictions, and instead sought simplistic answers to the world's challenges. Research into the psychology of those drawn to extremism finds that they think about the world in black and white, and struggle with complexity.[140] They are less able to regulate emotions, they are impulsive and seek evocative experiences such as brawling with counter-protesters and encountering law enforcement.

It wasn't until he was faced with the impact that his involvement in the NSM was having on others that the answers and solutions he sought in white nationalism no longer made sense. 'My family suffered. My kids suffered. My mom lost her career because of my involvement. I sacrificed my whole adult life to this garbage. My personal suffering is minimal compared to what I did. The work I do now is an attempt to repair the damage.'

Schoep's trajectory is fairly typical of those involved in right-wing extremism. His impetus for seeking out Nazism may be unique to him, but the search for community, meaning and black and white answers in a world of grey is not.

Schoep's story reflects the complex interplay between personal factors and structural conditions. An individual's path to violent extremism is a mix of ideological beliefs, involvement in extremist networks and personal grievances – what researchers refer to as 'needs, narratives and networks'.[141] But these personal motivations occur within a broader context. In my discussions with Schoep, he also referenced the alienating political and economic conditions of the post-Cold War environment of the early 1990s, when he came of age. He spoke about the 1994 North American Free Trade Agreement, the dramatic economic downturn in his home state of Michigan, and the accompanying loss of jobs and economic prospects.[142] He described an environment of scarcity where immigration was increasing and jobs were departing, threatening his already precarious sense of community and future potential. It was an environment in which he didn't feel confident that he or his 'in group' would succeed.

CHAPTER FOUR

The Great Replacement

Over time, Jeff Schoep's involvement in the NSM became less about his identification with Nazi history and neo-Nazi ideology. In fact, in his later days as leader, he removed the swastika from the NSM flag and branding. In his attempt to rebrand the NSM as part of the 'alt-right' instead of an explicitly neo-Nazi organisation, Schoep directed the NSM to focus on opposing immigration. He set up NSM 'patrols' along the Southwest border of the United States and recruited new members by convincing them that they were the only organisation that could 'do something' about the immigration they found so threatening.[143]

Again, Schoep's trajectory demonstrated the research evidence, that one of the most consequential predictors of support for right-wing extremism is a person's stance on immigration: how they believe it impacts national identity and their sense of belonging and status within society.[144]

This is not to say that if you have concerns about the social effects of new migrants and refugees, or if you advocate for lower migration intakes, you are a bigot or extremist.

However . . .

If you de-humanise migrants, you might be a right-wing extremist.

If you believe that increases in immigration and multicultural social models are part of a conspiracy to weaken 'native' society, you might be a right-wing extremist.

If you believe that 'certain types' of migrants can *never* assimilate, you might be a right-wing extremist.

If you adhere to a 'blood and soil' philosophy about the relationship of people to land, you might be a right-wing extremist.

At the very least, you would be participating in a long tradition of radical right thought around migration and immigrants, and parroting extreme-right conspiracies about the purpose and nature of immigration.

Hostility towards immigrants and refugees has long been a feature of right-wing extremist movements and far-right politics. But recent increases in migration and the resulting demographic shifts across Europe and in settler countries such as the United States, Canada, Australia and New Zealand have bolstered anxiety, insecurity and resentment in white-majority countries, which has in turn strengthened the appeal of right-wing extremist movements.

In the United States, for example, racial and ethnic minorities accounted for all of the nation's net population growth between 2010 and 2020. During that decade, for the first time ever, the white population declined as a percentage of the population.[145] These demographic shifts are portrayed by the far right as a threat to the white community. This majority-minority narrative has increased resentment towards growing non-white populations. It is also connected to the sense of economic dislocation discussed earlier and the perceived loss of status that comes with it.

More worryingly, it has turned some against democracy and electoral politics entirely, and into the arms of extreme-right movements. For status-anxious whites, the thinking goes that since they will soon be in the minority, they will no longer have the same sway over institutions, culture, society and politics.[146] Democracy will enable non-white empowerment at their expense.

Demographic shifts and the reactionary elements they provoke are not only occurring in America. In Europe, the so-called 'refugee crisis' of 2014–16 in which 1.3 million displaced people, mostly from Syria, Iraq and Afghanistan, arrived to seek asylum, undoubtedly contributed to the expansion of right-wing extremism.[147]

In Australia, overseas migration is the main source of population growth.[148] The latest statistics show that migration from Asia, primarily India and China, is driving this growth.[149] The Scanlon Foundation's Mapping Social Cohesion survey, Australia's longest-running national survey on social cohesion,[150] has measured increases in support for immigration and multiculturalism in its 2021 findings. This speaks to the health of Australia's multicultural society. But there are cracks. Islamophobia and negative attitudes towards Muslims remain persistently high.[151] Asian Australians also indicate that discrimination is a perpetual and growing issue, heightened during the pandemic.

Australia's far right has opportunities to capitalise on demographic shifts to polarise and radicalise, even when overall social cohesion is high. And right-wing extremist figures have most definitely done so. In addition to Asian and Muslim migrants, recent

African migrants and refugees have been targeted by Australian far-right figures.

Between 2015 and 2017, right-wing media and political figures who seized on statistics of growing crime among youth from African backgrounds – the children of recent refugees – cultivated an 'African crime' panic. With 2017 an election year, segments of the media and certain politicians saw an opportunity to manufacture a law-and-order crisis. The issue was used as a cynical ploy for votes and relevance. It eventually receded from the front pages and ended up being a losing election strategy, but damage was done. It marginalised the African refugee community and served up an opportunity for extremists to seize upon rhetoric in the media and by right-wing politicians about 'African gangs'. The extremists took it one step further than the politicians, blaming the government itself for allowing the migration that they framed as a threat to society.

Rallies organised by right-wing extremist figures in Melbourne during the height of the African gangs panic used the opportunity to protest against immigration and multiculturalism. 'Perhaps diversity isn't our greatest strength – perhaps all it's actually doing is dividing and destabilising our society,' far-right figure Blair Cottrell said in a message to followers promoting the rally.[152] In interviews on national television, Cottrell spread fear about young African migrants, claiming they were 'ransacking homes, carjacking, attacking police [and] chopping people up with machetes on the street'[153] in the northern suburbs of Melbourne.

*

Modern right-wing extremism frames immigration not just as an assault on 'native' populations, but also as part of a conspiracy. The so-called 'Great Replacement Theory' argues that increases in migration are not due to geopolitical, economic or environmental stresses driving desperate populations to seek refuge, but rather is part of a plot by a set of undefined elites working to replace native white or European people with minorities who they can better control.

The Great Replacement Theory was first articulated by French writer Renaud Camus in his 2011 book *Le Grand Remplacement*. Camus argues that white Europeans, particularly the French, are being replaced by non-white immigrants from Africa and the Middle East, and the result will be the erasure of French and European culture through the 'Islamification' of European societies.

Camus' articulation of the theory, based on ideas

rooted in early twentieth-century French ideologies and an earlier 'Eurabia' conspiracy theory, led him to be tried twice in France in 2019 for inciting racial hatred.[154] But this did not deter Camus, nor did it blunt the spread of the Great Replacement idea. Instead, an entire movement emerged that was centred on the Great Replacement: Génération Identitaire, or Generation Identity (GI).

GI took the Great Replacement Theory and developed a political and ideological program around it. GI, and the broader Identitarian movement it evolved from, advocates for the preservation of homogeneous ethno-cultural countries and is against migration and 'cultural mixing'. The movement promulgates the idea that multiculturalism is a scam and that integration and assimilation are impossible.

The Identitarian movement opened branches throughout Europe and garnered a large social media following.[155] GI embarked on a number of publicity stunts to raise its profile, such as the 'Defend Europe' campaign in which GI activists set sail on the Mediterranean in an attempt to block refugee rescue operations.[156] Along a snowy mountain pass in the French Alps, they unfurled banners that said, 'You will not make Europe your home. No way. Back to your homeland', while impersonating police officers and interfering in migrant crossings.[157]

The Identitarian movement has made inroads in Australia, where hardline, punitive policies against refugees and polarising immigration debates create fertile ground for such movements. European Identitarian movements have appropriated Australian slogans and approaches to immigration. For example, the 'You will not make Europe your home. No Way' slogan was lifted directly from the Australian Operation Sovereign Borders campaign under the Abbott government, in which Australian Navy vessels patrolled coastal waters to intercept people-smuggling boats carrying asylum seekers. Accompanying the operation was a communications campaign of YouTube videos and billboards aimed at potential asylum seekers, which featured the slogan, 'No way: You will not make Australia home.'[158] Extreme-right figures in Australia have also connected with the ethos of European Identitarianism.

*

The Identitarian movement has been at pains to portray itself as non-violent and part of the political mainstream. Far-right political parties in Europe have played coy with the movement, at certain points distancing themselves and at others repeating their talking points and appearing with GI figures.

Though GI describes itself as a non-violent, non-racist, patriotic nationalist movement, an Al Jazeera undercover investigation revealed that GI members were involved in and advocated for violence.[159] GI not only frames immigration as a type of invasion – an assault on white Europe by Muslims – it also offers a solution. It advocates 'remigration', or the forced deportation of non-native Europeans back to their supposed countries of origin.[160] 'Remigration' is essentially forced displacement. This call for action has directly incited violence, inspiring individuals to take matters into their own hands.

Al Jazeera's investigation captured one member of the Lille branch of GI laughing with his friends about his fantasy of committing a terrorist attack. 'The day I find out I have a terminal illness,' he says, 'I'll buy myself a weapon and cause carnage. I'm going to die anyway so I may as well be shot by the cops . . . A mosque, a car ramming, whatever . . . I'm going over there to cause carnage. It will make [the] Charlie Hebdo [shooting] look like a piece of piss.'[161]

This is not an empty threat. The Great Replacement idea featured in at least four recent right-wing terrorist mass shootings, including the attack against the Tree of Life synagogue in Pittsburgh, Pennsylvania in 2018, which killed 11. The El Paso, Texas mass shooter who killed 23 people in a Walmart store wrote about the Great Replacement idea in his manifesto and it influenced his choice of target – an 80 per cent Hispanic city.[162] The 2022 mass shooting in a predominantly African American community in Buffalo, New York by a right-wing extremist also referenced the Great Replacement Theory.

It was not only the idea of immigrant and minority takeover itself that influenced these violent acts, but the sense of existential threat that justifies and motivates urgent violent action. The US-based white supremacist website *The Daily Stormer* has a 'demographic countdown', which supposedly tracks the decline in the proportion of the global white population in real time. Grotesque antics such as these stoke a sense of urgency. The frequent and urgent reference to declining birth rates among the white or European population, or mass migration – what they frame as 'white genocide' – foster a panicked belief that white survival is under threat.

Most notoriously, the Great Replacement Theory played an integral part in the 2019 Christchurch attack. The title of Brenton Tarrant's 74-page manifesto was, in fact, 'The Great Replacement'. Pictures of Tarrant's weapons, which he posted on his Facebook page days before the attack, had 'the 14s' painted on them – a reference to a 14-word slogan written by neo-Nazi David Lane, well known among white supremacists for reflecting their existential concerns around the preservation of the white race. The Christchurch attacker also made donations to GI branches in Austria and France.[163]

Tarrant's manifesto discussed his travels in France, where 'in every French city, in every French town, the invaders were there'. He said his time in France led him to his decision to commit violence. 'There was a period of time two years prior to the attack that dramatically changed my views,' Tarrant wrote. 'These events turned my thoughts from pursuing a democratic, political solution and finally caused the revelation of the truth, that a violent, revolutionary solution is the only possible solution to our current crisis.' He explained that the defeat of far-right figure Marine Le Pen in the 2017 French election extinguished his hope in political activism to curb migration.

After being allowed to operate unfettered for years, enjoying close connections to Le Pen's National Rally and liaising with far-right and extreme-right influencers and movements globally, GI was finally shut down by the French state.[164] A detailed letter from the French Interior Ministry[165] instituting the group's sanction recognised it for what it was: a right-wing extremist movement. But by then, the harm was done.

Via mainstream and social media exposure of GI narratives and influencers, the Great Replacement conspiracy theory had polluted the mainstream.[166] In France, recent polls show that more than 60 per cent of people believe in some version of the Great Replacement Theory.[167] France's new far-right figure, Éric Zemmour, ran for the French presidency in 2022 on Great Replacement Theory talking points. Ironically, Zemmour is himself a descendant of migrant Algerian Jews and was raised, like many migrants, in the *banlieues* of Paris. He named his party Reconquest, which harkens back to the *Reconquista*, a period in history when Christian armies drove Muslims from Europe.

And while she did not win the 2022 presidential elections, Le Pen, who also embraced an anti-immigration, anti-Islam agenda, increased her share of the French vote, pulling in 41.5 per cent. It is emblematic of just how far to the right parts of France's electorate are turning and how fringe ideas are now firmly in the mainstream.[168]

But the Great Replacement Theory is not simply a French preoccupation.[169] It has been embraced by far-right and right-wing extremists globally.[170] It spread in the Anglosphere via Canadian influencer

Lauren Southern, a YouTube pin-up girl for the Great Replacement conspiracy theory, along with other far-right causes and movements.[171]

Southern first came to prominence via her online make-up tutorials that did double duty spewing anti-Muslim hate. But her sexy influencer persona belied a shrewd ability to promote a right-wing extremist agenda. Southern soon graduated from YouTube to making faux documentaries on the refugee crisis, publicising the antics of GI and Martin Sellner, the leader of GI's Austrian branch. Through a popular documentary she produced, Southern was largely responsible for publicising and promoting GI, Sellner and the Great Replacement Theory through-out Europe, North America and Australia.[172] She has also participated in speaking tours across continents.

In the United States, the Great Replacement Theory has gained traction thanks to Fox News commentator Tucker Carlson, who has referenced it ad nauseam on his show. A *New York Times* profile of Carlson revealed that he amplified the conspiracy theory that Democrats and elites want to force demographic change through immigration in more than 400 episodes of his show.[173] Carlson complains that the Democratic Party is attempting to 'replace the current electorate' or 'legacy Americans' with 'new people, more obedient voters from the third world', and that immigration is 'high enough to devalue your political power as a voter. It's high enough to subvert democracy itself. It's high enough to make this country a different place.'

While grievances and accusations about immigration have long been a feature of far-right politics, only recently have ideas around 'replacement' entered the American public discourse. Now, the accusation is that immigrants are not only out to steal jobs, but the 'very essence of America'.

An analysis by Media Matters for America found multiple and repeated references by other Fox News commentators and hosts to 'invasion' by migrants, the 'destruction' of society due to immigration and claims that immigration is part of a political plot by Democrats to seize power.[174] Florida Congressman Mike Gaetz has appeared on Fox News and writes on Twitter that 'there is an attempted cultural genocide going on in America right now . . . the left wants us to be ashamed of America so they can replace America'.[175]

It is no surprise that status anxiety fuelled by immigration was prevalent among participants in the 6 January Capitol siege.[176] University of Chicago political scientist Professor Robert Pape did a systematic study of the demographic profile and political geography of individuals arrested for their participation in the attack.[177] His study found that of all the individual demographic and geographic markers:

> Only one meaningful correlation emerged. Other things being equal, insurgents were much more likely to come from a county where the white share of the population was in decline. For every one-point drop in a county's percentage of non-Hispanic whites from 2015 to 2019, the likelihood of an insurgent hailing from that county increased by 25 per cent. This was a strong link, and it held up in every state . . . The insurgents could see their majority status slipping before their eyes.

By focusing on immigration rather than race, the Great Replacement Theory presents a racist idea through a veneer of non-racism. It allows far-right influencers to present their ideas about identity in a way that moves away from racial or ethnic hierarchies and superiorities. Instead, the Identitarian movement re-focuses the conversation to culture – namely the effects of migration on the degeneration of society and the erosion and ultimate extinction of the cultural majority.

Recent polling found that one in three Americans – both Republicans and Democrats – believe there is a concerted effort to replace natural-born US citizen votes with immigrant votes and that 'more immigration is causing US-born Americans to lose their economic, political and cultural influence'.[178]

This has allowed Great Replacement ideas to be more readily adopted by mainstream right-wing politicians.[179] While these figures would not necessarily endorse the violence promulgated by some Great Replacement Theory believers, 'they do suggest a conscious "dog-whistle" politics aimed at courting voters sympathetic to more extreme viewpoints, and underscore the extent to which fringe groups are able to influence mainstream political and public discourse around key wedge issues like migration.'[180]

What those who hawk the Great Replacement Theory fail or choose not to understand is that demography is *not* destiny. They are either misled by a narrative around demographic statistics that doesn't show the full picture, or they deliberately manipulate demographic and immigration statistics to justify their extremist views.

Author Arnon Grunberg puts it well:

Migration is not a crisis unless we are willing to call most of human history a crisis. The fact that we in Europe have come to use the term 'migration crisis' is partly because casting migration in a hostile light is still one of the most effective propaganda instruments of right-wing extremist parties.[181]

Demographic statistics indicating white population decline are also more nuanced than they appear. What the statistics do not show clearly is that while racial diversity is increasing at nationwide levels, it is also increasing at a micro level. There are more people with multi-racial identities and more young people consider themselves as belonging to more than one race, ethnicity and nationality. One in every nine babies born in America today will be from mixed-race families and this cohort will likely steadily grow.

So, instead of different non-white racial groups growing and competing for political, cultural and economic power, in fact, racial and ethnic groups are blending more than ever. Racial categories and identities are starting to make less and less sense.[182] Brenton Tarrant's objective in carrying out the Christchurch attack was to 'ensure the death of the "melting pot pipe dream"'.[183] Yet America may be finally living up to its moniker as the world's melting pot, and we can observe similar dynamics in other multicultural societies.

Demographic changes will *not* inevitably result in a zero-sum game between the races and to the marginalisation of whites. Rather, changing demographics reflect a greater racial blending. Demographic changes and cultural blending have happened throughout history in the United States and other immigrant societies such as Australia and Canada.

Moreover, to believe that these countries' identities and nationhood began with European settlement wilfully and ignorantly eradicates thousands of years of indigenous history. Australia is home to the world's oldest continuous civilisation – 60,000 years of Indigenous culture and history. If any group has an accurate claim to a 'great replacement' eradicating their communities, it is these indigenous populations.

Even in the so-called 'old world', generations of migrants have routinely shaped demography and culture. In France, where the Identitarian movement and the Great Replacement Theory got their start, the migration that the far right finds so alienating and threatening is rooted in France's colonial history. The vast majority of modern migrants to France come from former colonies where the French deliberately cultivated a sense of connection to the Republic among its colonial populations. France's inability to come to terms with its colonial legacy and its convoluted relationship with its past continues to be the source of marginalisation and confusion – for both its Gallic and migrant populations.[184]

But this is not just about white status anxiety or European cultural anxiety. Versions of the Great Replacement and concerns about immigration and refugees extend beyond white-majority countries. Nor is Islamophobia just a Western preoccupation. Europe and settler countries are not the only places around the world experiencing refugee crises and ethno-nationalist movements. Increasingly, Asia is beset by similar dynamics.

CHAPTER FIVE

Right-wing extremism in the East

Myanmar has gone through numerous transitions since its independence from British colonial rule. Since 1962, Myanmar has been ruled by military dictatorships with periodic attempts at representative governance in between. The country has suffered under often brutal rule and economic mismanagement, largely isolated from the international community, all while enduring ethnic minority insurgencies on multiple fronts. Only with the release of famed opposition leader and Nobel laureate Aung San Suu Kyi and the military's acquiescence to parliamentary elections in 2010 under a new quasi-democratic constitution did Myanmar end its international isolation and begin to undergo another attempt at democratic transition.

After a brief period of hope that the country was

on its way to resolving internal conflicts, loosening the military's hold over the economy and governance, and transitioning to democracy, since 2016 Myanmar has returned to volatility and violence. The emergence of Buddhist extremism co-opted by Myanmar's military, known as the Tatmadaw, ultimately led to what various International Criminal Court officials, human rights groups and governments including the United States labelled a genocide of Rohingya Muslims. It also led to a military coup and a rapid reversal of fortune for Aung San Suu Kyi, a global figure once considered the vessel for hopes of democracy and human rights in Myanmar, but now tainted by her denial that the military's campaign of violence against Rohingya communities amounted to ethnic cleansing. Aung San Suu Kyi is back under house arrest and the Tatmadaw is once again in control.

Though Myanmar is ethnically diverse, according to the last census, Buddhists make up 89.8 per cent of the population. Muslims likely make up just over four per cent of the population, although the latest census counts far fewer Muslims among Myanmar's population. The latest census figure does not include the estimated 1.2 million Rohingya present in Myanmar when the census was conducted in 2014.[185] Before the ethnic violence that took place in 2017, many Burmese Muslims were Rohingya. Non-Rohingya Muslims in Myanmar now almost certainly account for the majority of Muslims in the country. The Rohingya have lived in Myanmar for centuries but their status and political identity remain contested. Though they have held citizenship status in the past, for decades they have been considered neither Burmese citizens nor part of the *taing yin tha* – the 135 officially recognised ethnic groups that make up the Burmese nation. Instead of Rohingya, a term that is officially banned in Myanmar, they are referred to disparagingly as 'Bengali' to cement their outsider status.

In 2012, communal violence was sparked by the rape and murder of a Buddhist woman by a gang of Muslim men. The ensuing riots led to 200 deaths and 140,000 displaced people through the destruction of Muslim majority neighbourhoods in Rakhine State. The 2012 upsurge in anti-Muslim hate and communal violence was driven by a rise in chauvinistic, exclusionary Buddhist nationalism that was itself a product of the uncertainty and instability of Myanmar's political transition from a closed authoritarian state to a halting electoral democracy.[186] Buddhist extremism and the groups that promoted it were also deliberately cultivated by the Tatmadaw.

The unrest in Rakhine State was quickly taken up as a cause by an extremist monk, U Wirathu, leader of the 969 movement, a loose coalition of monks and lay people who promote themselves as a movement 'to preserve the teachings of the Buddha, the Dharma and the Sangha'.[187] Though they claimed to be for the promotion and preservation of Buddhism, they also fomented the idea that Buddhism was under threat from Islam and Muslims. They claimed that Bamar Buddhism was in dire need of protection because of a Muslim plot to take over the country enabled by a liberal, globally oriented, political elite. (Sound familiar?)

After the 2012 incident, Wirathu began ramping up his hate-filled sermons around the country, claiming Muslims were a threat not just in Rakhine but to Myanmar as a nation and to Buddhism as its majority religion. He preached that Buddhists were at risk of losing their majority due to high birth rates among Muslim communities. Muslim men were vilified as sexual predators targeting Buddhist women.[188] Wirathu's speeches and hateful propaganda circulated online and through the influence of the 969 movement's monks and welfare organisations.[189] He stoked a type of moral panic over the status of Buddhism with Muslims scapegoated for the troubles of Myanmar's transition. The group spread disinformation and rumours about the Muslim community and its supposed threat. One such rumour that sparked street violence, and was later found to be false, accused a Muslim business owner of raping their Buddhist employee.

In 2013, after growing international attention, 969 was banned for inciting violence. However, the movement simply rebranded and became a more centralised organisation with the backing of the military establishment.[191] Its new moniker was the Association for the Protection of Race and Religion, known by its Burmese-language acronym, MaBaTha.

MaBaTha continued its vilification of Muslims and incitement to violence. And in the process, it became politically influential, lobbying for legislation such as 'protection of race and religion' laws that gave government the power to implement population control measures in high density areas but that were targeted at Muslims in Rakhine State. They advocated for the Buddhist Women's Special Marriage Law, which requires submission of an application to the township registrar for any marriage of a Buddhist woman to a non-Buddhist man. And a Religious Conversion Law requiring anyone seeking to convert to another religion to apply for permission from the Religious Conversion Scrutinising and Registration Board.

These laws had a discriminatory intent against Muslims. Even though they violated constitutional provisions on religious freedom and the country's obligations under human rights conventions, the laws were passed under pressure from MaBaTha.

In 2016, MaBaTha was declared unlawful but it simply rebranded once again – this time as Buddha Dhamma Parahita Foundation. Attempts at banning the movement were ineffective and likely fuelled support for their ultra-nationalist exclusionary vision.[191] Through charitable works such as the distribution of food, shelter and medical care, they garnered trust and goodwill. Among majority Bamar Buddhists, the group was widely regarded not as extremist but as a broad-based social and religious movement dedicated to the protection of Buddhism during a time of unparalleled change and uncertainty. It was seen as upholding a traditional national identity in which Buddhism and the state were inseparable. The group was also viewed as a useful complement to Suu Kyi's National League for Democracy (NLD), which was respected and supported politically but which many Burmese thought was too Western in outlook.[192]

In 2017, the Arakan Rohingya Salvation Army, a Rohingya militant group designated a terrorist organisation by the Burmese government, staged a terrorist attack that pushed Rakhine State into renewed crisis. The attack seemed to justify all the extremist narratives about Muslims and their threat to the homeland. It also provided an opening for the Tatmadaw to claw back some power from the NLD following their historic electoral victory in 2015, using the attack to demonstrate that the Tatmadaw remained the only institution capable of safeguarding the integrity and Buddhist identity of the state and as pretext for a military campaign in Rakhine.

Soon after the attack, I visited Myanmar and had a rare opportunity to witness conditions first-hand in Rakhine, which was closed off to non-residents. I was able to visit the internally displaced persons (IDP) camps where most Rohingya Muslims had been forced to reside since 2012. After establishing these camps and forcing the Rohingya population into them, the military and government abandoned all responsibility for administration and provision of services. Conditions inside the camps were dire and undignified. Malnutrition, poor sanitation and violence abounded.

Though international aid agencies were doing their best to assist, it was clear as I walked around the camps that these were, in the plainest of terms, government-sponsored concentration camps whose administration had been subcontracted to NGOs. Just as outsiders were not allowed to enter without permission, the occupants of these camps were not allowed to leave without permission. That permission was rarely granted, thus denying the occupants access to schools, markets, hospitals and basic health services.[193] At the time of my visit, families had been stuck in these camps for five years.

The Myanmar government was essentially conducting an incremental ethnic cleansing, hoping that the inhabitants of the camps would dissolve back into the earth and the remaining Rohingya villagers would die or cross into Bangladesh. International NGOs were left to pick up the pieces. It was a disturbing and tragic situation that only became worse.

I had been in Myanmar in January 2017, and by August the Tatmadaw had launched another military campaign against the Rohingya after the Arakan Rohingya Salvation Army attacked police and army posts. The Tatmadaw mounted a brutal campaign. The United Nations Human Rights Council report on the atrocities found that the military conducted its operations in Rakhine with 'genocidal intent'.[194] They conducted mass killings, raped Rohingya women and assaulted children. Under conservative estimates, 10,000 Rohingya were killed and more than 700,000 were forced to flee to neighbouring countries, mainly Bangladesh.[195] This was all done with the broad support of the majority Bamar Buddhist community, the acquiescence of the NLD and the silence of Aung San Suu Kyi.

There is no doubt that the 2017 genocide was committed with the encouragement of ultra-nationalists and MaBaTha supporters, who had prepared the ground by stoking anti-Muslim sentiment for years. But what drove the Rohingya genocide and mass displacement in Myanmar is rarely labelled right-wing extremism. Rather, it is portrayed as sectarian conflict between ethnic communities, a crisis manufactured by the Tatmadaw to retain its hold on power, or part of the often ugly process of nation building. It is indeed all those things, but I would argue that it should also be understood as part of a broader global right-wing extremist movement connected to rising Islamophobia.

Right-wing extremism is present not only in the West but in the Global South. Buddhist extremism possesses all of the ingredients of right-wing extremism defined in earlier chapters: exclusionary ethno-nationalism, conspiratorial beliefs, hostility to democracy, notions of racial or religious supremacy, and the justification of violence. The ethnic cleansing in Myanmar was conducted by the Tatmadaw, who held views and acted in ways that reflected fascist ideology and behaviour. MaBaTha was not unlike white supremacist movements in the West, which advocate for an ethno-nationalist state to preserve the purity of their race, ethnicity or religion.[196]

Examining these movements through the lens of right-wing extremism also highlights the key role that Islamophobia plays. Islamophobia does not just manifest itself in the West. Arguably, it manifests just as strongly in Asia. The MaBaTha and other Buddhist extremists sequestered, vilified and persecuted an outsider group of Rohingya Muslims, spreading rhetoric about the dangers of the Muslim threat and claimed that Burmese Buddhism was under siege from Islam. Like other extreme right-wing movements, it was 'Islamophobic, ethnocentric and chauvinistic in its preaching'.[197] It predicated itself on the targeting and scapegoating of an 'out group' – Muslim minorities – in the name of protecting an 'in group' and upholding Buddhist nationalism.

For those of us used to associating Buddhism with a certain equanimity, calm and the interconnectedness of life, it can be jarring to encounter Buddhist extremism. Instead of repeating mantras of loving kindness, there are extreme ethno-nationalist Buddhist monks such as Wirathu who cry, 'Now is not the time for calm . . . Now is the time to rise up, to make your blood boil.'[198] Wirathu calls himself 'the Burmese bin Laden' and was labelled 'the face of Buddhist terror' on the cover of *Time* magazine.

What complicates matters in discussing Buddhist extremism in Myanmar is that these 'extremist' positions had broad and popular support. It is an instructive example of how extremism can take hold of a society and its politics under the right conditions. Buddhist supremacists managed to accomplish what white supremacists in the West have only macabrely dreamed of doing: following their Nazi predecessors to orchestrate the erasure of minorities and perceived enemies. Buddhist supremacist extremism led to an actual genocide.

*

These dynamics are not confined to Myanmar. They are at play throughout Asia.[199] In Sri Lanka, Buddhist ethno-nationalist and supremacist movements such as the Bodu Bala Sena (BBS) advocate for an exclusionary Buddhist identity, also with the collusion and cooperation of governing elites.[200] Anti-Muslim sentiment is widespread in Sri Lanka and is weaponised by movements such as the BBS, who constantly claim traditional Sinhalese Buddhist practices would be 'outlawed' in Muslim-majority countries. They equate Muslims as a whole with

ISIS and claim, in the words of BBS leader Galagoda Aththe Gnanasara, that Muslims 'are now prepared to destroy us'.

BBS claims that formerly Buddhist-majority countries such as Afghanistan, Bangladesh and Pakistan are now Muslim majority due to Islamic invasion in past centuries and warn that Sri Lanka could be the next domino to fall.[201] They have presented Sri Lankan Muslims as an insider threat, staged a campaign of intimidation aimed at individuals who convert to Islam and have pressured the state to respond to spurious complaints of actions against Buddhist identity. All the while, authorities have displayed an almost total lack of action against Buddhist extremists.[202]

Buddhist extremist groups in Sri Lanka are not only using coded language and fear-mongering. Gnanasara has called for violence explicitly, including the stoning to death of Muslims. He was responsible for two anti-Muslim pogroms, in June 2014 and March 2018.

Like their right-wing counterparts in the West, BBS also rails against multiculturalism and secularism, warning that if Sri Lankan secularism and multicultural tolerance is taken too far it will provide an opportunity for an Islamic takeover.[203] And like other right-wing extremist groups, BBS makes frequent use of disinformation and conspiracy theories, such as spreading rumours that Muslim-owned restaurants were injecting sterilisation medicine into food to suppress the fertility of the Sinhalese Buddhist majority, supposedly to assist in their stealth takeover of the country through higher birth rates.[204]

The 2019 Easter bombing by Islamic State affiliates provided a further opening for Buddhist extremist groups to expand their appeals and gave them greater prominence in affairs of state. Muslim leaders were targeted. There were calls for the resignations of Muslim government ministers, officials, lawyers and rights activists.[205] Gnanasara was appointed to a presidential task force on anti-discrimination and human rights despite his very public record of vilification.

*

In India, there is growing anti-Muslim sentiment through the rise of Hindutva extremism – an ideology that seeks to dismantle India's multicultural and secular state and argues that India should be considered a solely Hindu nation, relegating India's non-Hindu population to second-class citizens. Hindutva extremism is deeply intertwined with the populist far-right politics of Indian Prime Minister Narendra Modi and the governing Bharatiya Janata

Party (BJP).[206] Manifestations of Hindutva have led to violence, hate speech and vilification of Indian Muslims in particular.

Hindutva should be considered a 'variant' of right-wing extremism.[207] Extremism researcher Eviane Leidig, who has examined the Hindutva movement in the context of right-wing extremism, quotes Madhav Sadashiv Golwalkar, leader of the paramilitary Hindu nationalist Rashtriya Swayamsevak Sangh (RSS), who offers an unambiguous articulation of Hindu superiority and describes what his proposed obliteration of Indian multiculturalism would mean for Indian minorities:

> The foreign races in Hindusthan [India] must . . . entertain no ideas but those of the glorification of the Hindu race and culture . . . [they] must lose their separate existence to merge in the Hindu race, or may stay in the country, wholly subordinated to the Hindu Nation, claiming nothing, deserving no privileges, far less any preferential treatment – not even citizen's rights. There is, at least should be, no other course for them to adopt.[208]

Historically, extremist Hindu and Nazi connections go beyond the latter's appropriation of the swastika. RSS founding fathers were influenced by

German and Italian fascism. They even travelled to meet with Mussolini in Italy and openly supported the Third Reich, bonding over their shared connection of promoting Aryan superiority. They promoted a similar militarised fascism for India and likened the Muslims of India to the Jews of Germany. There were a number of cultural, political and educational exchanges and networks between the fascist regimes of Europe and the RSS and Hindutva movement in the 1930s and 40s. They shared a belief in the concept of group or civilisational superiority based on inherent racial characteristics.

Like European fascists, Hindutva adherents promoted a version of 'blood and soil', arguing that being Hindu 'was a matter of race and blood' geographically bound to India.[209] Hindutva's founding ideological text, written by V. D. Savarkar and first published in 1923, defines the nation according to an 'unconditionally ethnic Hindu-ness and territorial belonging'. Like the Burmese MaBaTha and the Sri Lankan BBS, the Hindutva movement pulled at the threads of their country's multicultural tapestry, constructing an exclusionary Indian identity, extolling Hindus as 'real Indians' and casting non-Hindus, mainly Muslims, as outsiders and usurpers.[210]

Unsurprisingly, this led to pogroms against Muslims in India and other forms of communal and targeted violence. Indeed, Mahatma Gandhi was assassinated by a former RSS member for his call for 'Hindu–Muslim unity' in the aftermath of the Great Partition.

Hindutva has found expression in many different forms and movements in India, but primarily through the RSS and the BJP. The BJP was founded around the time of Indian independence and was opposed to the pluralistic, secular Indian National Congress, a party based on Gandhi's vision for India and helmed by the Nehru dynasty for decades. The BJP rejected Gandhian ideas of pluralism and diversity and advocated for an exclusionary Hindu nationalism. It later exploited the common perception of the Congress Party as a dynastic, sclerotic elite, out of touch with the average Indian.

Hindutva took off in the early 1990s when Hindu mobs organised by the RSS destroyed the Babri Masjid mosque in Ayodhya. Accompanying riots killed thousands of Muslims.[211] The movement gained greater traction with the rise of Narendra Modi. In Modi, who has a long history of involvement with the Hindutva movement, these extremists have a champion for their Hindu nationalist goals. Modi relies heavily on Hindutva to reinforce his populist appeal. He also came up through the RSS, a key component of the ruling BJP.

Modi personally has a problematic history with violence and incitement. Though he denies it, he remains accused of having a role in the 2002 anti-Muslim pogroms in Gujarat, which lasted for weeks and led to more than a thousand, mostly Muslim, deaths. Reports by journalists and human rights groups implicated state officials, including Modi, then BJP Chief Minister, who they accused of working alongside RSS affiliates to orchestrate and plan the attacks. A minister in Modi's government, since murdered in 2003, accused Modi of explicitly instructing civil servants and police not to stand in the way of the mob attacking Muslims.[212] Until his election as prime minister, Modi was barred from entry to the United Kingdom, the United States and Europe because of his involvement in these events.

Under Modi's leadership, Islamophobia and right-wing Hindu supremacism have grown and become more mainstream. So too have violence and communal tensions. There have been increased incidents of mobs violently attacking and intimidating Muslim businesses. Hindu extremists have confronted Muslims during Friday prayers. Vigilantes have targeted Muslims via lynching campaigns.[213]

Disinformation has spread about a campaign of so-called 'love jihad' – a conspiracy theory that Muslim men are luring Hindu women into marriage to convert them to Islam as a means of ensuring future Muslim dominance over Hindus.[214] It has prompted murders and other vigilante violence against Muslim men suspected of being in interfaith relationships. Several BJP-controlled states have enacted legislation thwarting interfaith marriages, which has led to the arrests of hundreds of men.[215]

Hindutva can no longer be considered extreme in India. It has become mainstream. It is considered normal and legitimate to hold Hindu supremacist views. As Leidig succinctly puts it, 'There is currently a right-wing extremist party governing the world's largest democracy, yet [acknowledgement of this] . . . is remarkably absent.'[216]

What does this bode for the world's largest democracy? The rise of Hindutva under Modi and the emboldening of extremists is eroding India's secular democracy and its multicultural identity. In democracy rankings, India under Modi has been downgraded to only 'partly free'.[217]

Critics of the RSS and the BJP who have tried to hold them to account for their incitement of violence and human rights abuses are subjected to online and real-world intimidation campaigns. Activists critical of Modi have been threatened with prosecution under questionable anti-terrorism legislation.[218] Funding has been pulled from news outlets that won't cover Modi sycophantically or parrot exclusionary Hindu nationalist sentiment. India's Islamic history is being erased from schoolbooks.[219]

The Modi government also revoked Article 370 of the Constitution, removing the special status of the disputed territories region of Jammu and Kashmir. It was a highly controversial move that fulfilled the Hindutva movement's ambition to fully restore the territory to India.[220]

Through the Citizenship Amendment Act, the BJP created exclusionary exceptions to citizenship based on religion, fundamentally challenging the secular and inclusive ideals India was founded on. The Indian government has been accused of targeting Muslims through recent legislation regarding the National Register of Citizens, which seeks to detain and remove 'illegal' Muslim residents. The justification? The government claims that millions of illegal Muslim 'infiltrators' have crossed into India from neighbouring countries. If those detained are eventually to be expelled from India, it would trigger a forced migration larger than the Rohingya crisis.

There are dire predictions that conditions are ripe for a campaign of targeted violence against 'non-citizens' in India on the same scale as that in Myanmar.[221] At Hindu right-wing rallies and other public forums, Hindu extremists speak approvingly of the genocide in Myanmar and encourage India to do the same: 'Just like Myanmar, the police in this nation, the army, the politicians and every Hindu must join hands, pick up their weapons and carry out this cleanliness drive.'[222]

CHAPTER SIX

The globalised extreme right

Norwegian right-wing extremist Anders Breivik, who killed 77 people in a terrorist attack in 2011, wrote in his manifesto, 'It is essential that the European and Indian resistance movements learn from each other and cooperate as much as possible. Our goals are more or less identical.'[223] Recently, Western right-wing extremists have obliged. British right-wing extremists are adopting hate campaigns developed by Hindu extremists.[224] British right-wing extremist influencers have been copying hashtags and disseminating memes accusing Muslims of deliberately spreading coronavirus, some of them taken directly from the social media accounts of Bharatiya Janata Party (BJP) ministers.[225] American right-wing conspiracy website InfoWars has replicated hashtags and conspiracy theories that began in India. European radical right figures have travelled to the annexed territory of Kashmir. The Kashmir issue has become a rallying point for far-right figures in Europe who look to Modi as a model for what can be done when a far-right ethno-nationalist leader takes power.[226]

Right-wing extremists and far-right movements have always cooperated across borders,[227] despite the conventional wisdom that they are nationally oriented and locally focused. Even white supremacist groups are looking to other ethnicities and countries for inspiration, such as India, where exclusivist Hindu nationalism has taken hold and the caste system is being held up as an example to justify human hierarchies. Or Japan – a country white supremacists extol as an exemplar society that has maintained its racial purity and not succumbed to multiculturalism – which is also experiencing an increase in far-right nationalism.[228]

But over the past decade, the scene has undergone an accelerated process of internationalisation.[229] Right-wing extremists are increasingly convinced they must organise globally to meet global challenges. There has been more frequent cooperation among right-wing extremist actors and organisations across borders as well as a common conceptualisation and narrative of a global struggle and shared goals that extend beyond national boundaries.[230]

One unifying narrative that has emerged globally is of a white civilisation and white race in decline, and the need to defend it. It has become a goal that right-wing extremists in traditionally white-majority multicultural countries are now striving for and uniting behind.[231] As the propaganda material of Combat 18, a neo-Nazi brand that started in the United Kingdom in 1992, puts it, 'Our National Socialist family now transcends national borders, we do not owe our allegiance to any nation, our only allegiance is to our race – The White Race. Our countries are just geographical areas in which we just happen to live, but our race knows no national boundaries in this eternal struggle.'[232] Ironic, given Combat 18's 'blood and soil' beliefs and anti-immigration stance.

But now, when right-wing extremists conjure the slogan 'blood and soil', they are likely to use it in reference to their defence of a 'global white race' as much as to their own lands. As one study of the globalisation of the extreme right summarised the situation:

Whether it is American neo-Nazis concerned about the growth of the non-white share of the population or European right-wing extremists who believe in the theory of 'the great replacement' or Russian ultra-nationalists who feel that their traditional 'white'

culture is being threatened by Western multiculturalism, gay rights, and the like, many have come to
the same conclusion: that they need to defend themselves, that it might be useful to cooperate in order
to do so, and that the means by which this conflict
will be resolved will be a civil war-like scenario . . .
envisaged as a global, transnational conflict.[233]

Though formal cross-border organisational ties
and networking are important aspects of the globalisation of right-wing extremism, just as important are
the transnational cultural and sporting events and
international speaking tours and conventions that
bind ties among extremists.

Mixed martial arts (MMA) has emerged as
the sport du jour. Right-wing extremist groups in
different countries – such as White Rex, which
originated in Russia, and the Rise Above Movement
(RAM), which started in the United States – converge
at MMA tournaments. Germany is also host to
international MMA events such as the 'Battle of the
Nibelungs'. American MMA groups such as RAM
have not only participated in German MMA events
but sought to emulate their European counterparts
by blending martial arts, sport, merchandising and
extremist ideology.[234] All attract people from around
the world.[235]

Music festivals and rallies from Germany to Greece to Ukraine help establish links across countries and serve as safe spaces for right-wing extremists to loudly '*Sieg Heil*' to death metal or racist rap.[236] In Germany, the *Schild und Schwert* (Shield and Sword) music festival in Ostritz and the *Rock gegen Überfremdung* (Rock against Over-foreignisation) concert series are attended by extremists from all over Europe and the Americas, and serve as an important source of revenue for their movements.[237]

A cohort of globally recognised right-wing extremist ideologues and influencers travel and network via speaking tours. Through events and conventions, bolstered by their online presence, they promote shared narratives and facilitate a growing ideological convergence among national right-wing extremist groups.

There is a consolidation of global enemies: multiculturalism, LGBTQI rights, feminism, the amorphous 'global elite', Jews, Muslims, antifa and liberal democratic governments. The extreme right now also derives those enemies, narratives and grievances from outside their local and national context. What happens in one country can inflame tensions, exacerbate grievances and justify narratives and ideologies among right-wing extremists in another.

For example, Australian right-wing extremists discuss the Black Lives Matter movement in the United States as justification for their ideological beliefs. European immigration and refugee issues are being referenced and discussed in Canada and the United States as if they were happening within their own borders. Right-wing extremists are connecting their own nation's political and societal failings to the machinations of a global cabal. Anti-Semitic New World Order conspiracy theories permeate right-wing extremist movements around the globe.

The centrality of US right-wing discourse among right-wing extremist movements is clear. The Institute for Strategic Dialogue, a UK think tank focusing on extremism, polarisation and disinformation, tracked the online posts of extremists from across the English-speaking world and found that 'extremists in Canada were focused nearly as much on US [politics] as they were on their own domestic politics'. They found a similar pattern in Australia and New Zealand. 'What's happening in America has an out weighted effect on the English-speaking extremist landscape. Events which happen in America serve to energise and mobilise extremists internationally.'[238]

Right-wing conspiracy theories are also being repurposed. For example, the Big Lie conspiracy theory around electoral fraud in the US presidential election that motivated the 6 January 2021 insurrection was recycled in the United Kingdom, where far-right actors spread conspiracy theories in the lead-up to the London mayoral elections in May that year.[239]

There is still division and competition among right-wing extremist and far-right groups.[240] Some extremists continue to privilege their national struggle. And attempts at global integration have not been without friction.[241] It is also true that right-wing extremist organisations are often unstructured, diverse or splintered, and organisationally disunited,[242] even within their own domestic spheres of operation.[243] Many right-wing extremist groups – particularly white supremacist movements in the West – have a history of forming, collapsing and reorganising, so it is tempting to think of them as unstable.

However, the white supremacist movement needs to be examined as a whole.[244] These organisations are fluid formations that form part of a broader network. Often the same cast of characters reconfigure into new groups and networks. And as will be discussed in the next chapter, many right-wing extremist movements have adopted a deliberate strategy of avoiding hierarchical membership organisations, operating instead 'as a network of small, underground cells, each with a high degree of autonomy',[245] yet with the intention to 'unify militant[s] around the globe'.[246]

Meanwhile, the transnationalisation of right-wing extremism is happening. Formerly nationally focused groups such as Sweden's Nordic Resistance Movement, the Russian Imperial Movement, Greece's Golden Dawn, France's Identitarian movement, Germany's *Der III. Weg*, or the United States' Atomwaffen Division (now known as the National Socialist Order) have become more global in outlook. Atomwaffen Division was initially connected to an international neo-Nazi network referred to as the 'global fascist fraternity', which grew out of an online forum called Iron March.[247] These groups are now the core of what some are labelling the 'Brown International',[248] a reference to Hitler's Brownshirts, a Nazi paramilitary organisation officially known as the *Sturmabteilung (SA)* or Storm Troopers.

The Nordic Resistance Movement (NRM), the largest neo-Nazi movement in Northern Europe and itself a merger of multiple Scandinavian right-wing extremist groups, is considered a role model by the broader right-wing extremist milieu for its international outreach and expansion efforts.[249]

On its open access website – helpfully navigable in multiple languages – the NRM posts editorials in its news section on how 'transnational connections strengthen the resistance movement',[250] as well as honours for 'fallen comrades' from other right-wing extremist movements[251] and interviews with NRM leader Simon Lindberg discussing how the global order has compelled them to work transnationally:

> If they're working to ensure that we have less international cooperation, we should probably work extra hard to expand such cooperation and make these relationships even closer, since this would really benefit us. We live in an increasingly global world in which national borders are becoming less and less important. This is not something we want; on the contrary, it is a part of something we fight against. However, we must also adapt to the prevailing reality. This is an important part of why we have always fought actively for a united Nordic region and not just for a sovereign Sweden. This means that international cooperation can undoubtedly become even more important in the future.[252]

Other right-wing extremist groups have taken notice. National Action, a neo-Nazi movement proscribed as a terrorist organisation in the United Kingdom, looked to the NRM's transnational outreach as a model and sought to become a spoke in right-wing extremist international networks. Members took part in rallies and met and trained with other like-minded extremists in other countries.[253] German neo-Nazis and right-wing extremists – among the most internationally networked of all the cohorts[254] – have developed more connections with other European, American and Russian movements. German extremist movement *Die Rechte* has sent its members to speak at events organised by violent right-wing organisations worldwide.

The NRM was also lauded by American extremist Matthew Heimbach, a key organiser of the white supremacist Unite the Right rally in Charlottesville in 2017, who was indicted for conspiracy for his role in the violence. Heimbach called the NRM a 'vanguard' in the national socialist movement. The NRM in turn called for a more coordinated transatlantic approach with US far-right extremists.[255] Answering the call, Heimbach travelled repeatedly to Europe to meet with counterparts to network, fundraise and strategise. In an interview with *The New York Times*, Heimbach described how his European sojourns gave him ideas for making the white nationalist movement in the United States a 'real political force' and validated his efforts to 'create a broader, world-wide network'.[256]

RUSSIA'S ROLE

Difficult as it is to fathom, given Russia's central role in defeating Nazi Germany, Russian connections to neo-Nazi movements and other right-wing extremists around the world are many. Even as Russian President Vladimir Putin wages a war of naked aggression against Ukraine based on a flimsy predicate of 'denazification'[257], neo-Nazis, ultra-nationalists and white supremacists look to Russia as the last bulwark against the decaying liberal West's turn to post-modern progressivism and corruption.

One examination of Russia's role concluded that it is 'running an active-measures campaign to culti-vate right-wing support to undermine the West'.[258] It is doing so in typically opaque Russian fashion, through various actors and methods including 'the Kremlin, covert branches of the state, regime-linked oligarchs and state-tolerated right-wing groups in Russia itself that sometimes work with the govern-ment but at times oppose it'.[259]

President Putin is considered by right-wing extremists as a guardian of Western civilisation. He is admired for his strongman persona and sup-posed resistance to the encroaching corruption and decadence of Western societies. He is perceived as a defender of traditional values and an opponent of the LGBTQI rights that threaten the traditional family. He is the last line of defence against Islamist threats and crusher of corrupt elitist global institutions such as the European Union (EU), the North Atlantic Treaty Organization (NATO) and the United Nations (UN). Putin's conceptualisation of nationhood and statehood – ethnically based and autocratic – is also compatible with the far right and stands in contrast to the liberal idea of a state based on civic responsibility, rule of law and individual rights.[260]

Russian information campaigns have amplified right-wing extremist discourse and narratives around immigration, government corruption and threats from the left, helping to bolster mainstream exposure of these ideas. Russia's Facebook equivalent, VK, has welcomed extremists after they were deplatformed by Facebook and other social media outlets. Russian intelligence services sponsor fight clubs in multiple European countries, which have been used to spread Russian influence and act as a liaison point for extreme right-wing actors.[261]

Russia has also sought to cultivate white supremacist movements such as the Atomwaffen Division and The Base. An investigative report by *The Guardian* and the BBC revealed that The Base's leader, Rinaldo Nazzaro, moved from the United States to St Petersburg in 2018. Russia also has links to Matthew Heimbach, who says, 'Russia is our biggest inspiration' and that he and many other extremist colleagues consider Vladimir Putin 'the leader of the free world'.[262]

Russia has used the Russian Orthodox Church in its cultivation of right-wing extremists. The Russian Orthodox Church Outside Russia (ROCOR) has attracted a number of right-wing extremist figures. Conversion into Eastern Orthodox Christianity has become a trend within the far right – particularly among white supremacists, neo-traditionalists and male supremacists. It is a trend that is both aided and encouraged by the Russian state.[263]

Russia has played host to the so-called 'World National Conservative Movement' (WNCM), an international association sponsored by the Russian political party Rodina that organises against the principles of 'liberalism, multiculturalism and tolerance', which they have identified, along with globalisation, as leading to the 'erosion of nations . . . the falling away from religion, replacement of spirituality by materialism, impoverishment of cultures, [and the] destruction of the family and healthy moral values'.[264] The list of WNCM members is a who's who of right-wing extremists and far-right political party players, which includes organisations mostly from Europe and the United States but also Chile, Japan, Mongolia, Syria and Thailand.[265]

One Russian emissary cultivating transnational right-wing extremism is the Russian Imperial Movement (RIM), which has the distinction of being the first right-wing extremist group placed on the US State Department's Foreign Terrorist Organizations list. It has since been proscribed as an international terrorist organisation by other Western governments. The RIM is a paramilitary unit that, according to its spokesperson, seeks 'to establish contacts with right-wing, traditionalist and conservative organisations around the world . . . to share the experience of political [and] information warfare and joint squad tactics training'[266] and has been connected to right-wing extremist plots and activities in Europe.[267]

There is a Russian connection to the Australian far right, too. A marginal pro-Kremlin group called the Zabaikal Cossack Society of Australia considers Australia to be a 'hostile state'. It has mounted demonstrations in support of Russian separatist claims in Crimea, clashed with Ukrainians in Australia and intimidated the Russian community in Australia when it has displayed insufficient allegiance to Putin.[268] The group also associates with other Australian white supremacist figures and Australian members of Greek neo-Nazi movement Golden Dawn. Its leadership has reportedly travelled to Ukraine to liaise with pro-Russian forces. An ABC News report confirmed that its members have spent time with separatists involved in Russian-supported battalions in eastern Ukraine and met with others who are subject to Australian government sanctions.[269]

There are reports of at least five Australians fighting for Russian-backed militias in Ukraine. Ukrainian officials notified the Australian government and pushed for the individuals to be charged under counter-terrorism legislation.[270] However, because their movements were not proscribed under Australian law, the men were free to return home and did not face charges.

The Base's Rinaldo Nazzaro has conducted global recruitment from his Russian base, including in Australia. In 2021, the ABC obtained secret tape recordings of Nazzaro vetting potential Australian recruits to the cause, including one who had aspired to federal parliament and run as a candidate for the far-right One Nation Party. On the phone call, Nazzaro bemoaned the fact that The Base did not yet have a presence in Australia: 'We have barely a toehold right now in Australia, we need to change that to a foothold.'

He would attempt to do so via a structured recruitment drive that targeted young people and those with firearms training, military or security experience and known associations with right-wing extremist groups.[271] Soon after this reporting, the Australian government listed The Base as a proscribed terrorist organisation.[272]

UKRAINE: A LOCUS FOR THE EXTREME RIGHT

Given the recent history of the Islamic State caliphate and the role of foreign combatants in Afghanistan, we often associate foreign fighters with jihadism. And indeed, the transnationalisation of jihadism offers a useful, if not entirely analogous, example of how various domestic right-wing extremist groups are coalescing into a global movement via foreign conflicts.

In the 1980s, the Afghan insurgency against the Soviet occupation became central to the emergence of a new type of transnational violent extremist movement. While the Afghan conflict was primarily a domestic insurgent movement against a foreign occupying force, it also became the nucleus of global jihadism.

At the time, the Afghan conflict was one of the most successful mobilisations of Muslim volunteer foreign fighters, with an estimated 35,000 Islamists travelling to Afghanistan to participate in the fight against the Soviets.[273] It would be only slightly surpassed by the mobilisation to the Islamic State caliphate in Syria in 2015. The Afghan insurgency epitomised the struggle to liberate Muslim lands from non-Muslim influence. It became a vector for a litany of Muslim grievances against the West and its various Middle Eastern allies.[274] The fight to preserve Afghanistan from the godless Soviets eventually spawned the creation of al-Qaeda and charted a new direction for the jihadist cause.

For many years, jihadists in the Middle East concentrated their efforts and attacks against their own governments and religious establishments – what they called the 'near enemy'. But they were met with repression and a lukewarm response from their own societies. After coalescing in Afghanistan, they embarked on a new strategy via al-Qaeda ideologues, who articulated a need to focus on the 'far enemy' – first the Soviet Union and then the United States and its Western allies.[275] Afghanistan combined its individual, nationalistic, revolutionary struggles into a broader global movement with the goal of erasing national boundaries in the Muslim world, creating a worldwide caliphate of the global Muslim *ummah*.

Just as Afghanistan was critical to the formation of transnational jihadism, the 2014 Donbas conflict in Ukraine, the annexation of Crimea, and the 2022 Russian invasion of Ukraine have been important to the transnationalisation of the extreme right. Like the jihadists before them, right-wing foreign fighters would now 'no longer subscribe to the narrow concept of nationalism but instead imagine themselves as participating in a global struggle against a global enemy'.[276]

The analogy is not exact. There is no right-wing extremist equivalent to al-Qaeda emerging out of Ukraine. The foreign fighter situation there is murkier; unlike Afghanistan, right-wing extremist foreign fighters have fought on both sides of the Russia–Ukraine conflict, and not all the foreign fighters who flocked to participate in the war are right-wing extremists.[277]

Yet interviews with foreign fighters conducted by Polish researcher Kacper Rekawek reveal a marked unity in viewpoints among extreme right-wing foreign fighters. According to Rekawek, they are 'fatalistic about the future of the West/Europe/their country due to a multitude of factors, such as alleged corruption, what they call the liberal *diktat*, or their perception of American imperialism, cultural Marxism'.[278] Regardless of whether they were on the side of Russian separatists or Ukrainian militias, there was a common belief in anti-liberalism, antagonism towards democratic states, anti-elitism, anti-Semitism, a sense of traditionalism and support for patriarchal family structures, and opposition to LGBTQI, leftist and feminist ideas.[279]

In a sense, it did not matter that they were fighting each other. Their choice of which side to fight for was governed more by who they knew rather than any significant ideological differences.[280] In fact, some fighters, such as those from the Scandinavian NRM, first started on one side of the conflict (Ukrainian) and then switched to the other (Russian, now with strong ties to the RIM).[281] Even as right-wing extremist foreign fighters battled each other, the conflict served to consolidate a right-wing extremist worldview, validated the transnationalisation of the cause and provided a venue for networking and interaction. As one of Rekawek's interviewees put it, they became part of a 'Western foreign fighter society'.[282]

One group in the conflict that has attracted and recruited a number of foreign fighters and gained international attention is the Azov Battalion. The group fought effectively on the front lines against pro-Russian separatists in Donetsk in eastern Ukraine and grew out of a movement called the Right Sector. They helped liberate Mariupol in 2014 from Russian separatists. Their professionalism and effectiveness made Azov the best volunteer unit in the eyes of Ukraine's Interior Ministry.[283] As a result, the Azov Battalion was incorporated into the Ukrainian National Guard and is now known as the Azov Regiment. It is part of the government security services defending Ukraine against Putin's 2022 invasion.[284]

The unit was initially formed out of the ultra-nationalist Patriot of Ukraine organisation and the neo-Nazi Social-National Assembly (SNA). The group continues to use Nazi symbols for its insignia. Its members have perpetrated violence against the Roma and LGBTQI communities. Founder Andriy Biletsky reportedly said that Ukraine's national purpose is to 'lead the white races of the world in a final crusade . . . against Semite-led *Untermenschen* [inferior races]'.[285] Biletsky's nickname within the group is Bely Vozhd, or White Ruler.[286] Members of the Azov Battalion have also been accused of committing human rights abuses, including torture.[287]

Azov has attracted extremist foreign fighters from around the world. It has a 'Western outreach office' where it recruits from fight clubs and neo-Nazi music festivals, and it has cultivated relationships with white supremacists around the world.[288] Even though it did appear at various times on Facebook's banned 'Dangerous Individuals and Organizations' list, the group was able to use the platform to recruit foreign fighters to Ukraine.[289]

Individuals from the United States, Europe and Australia have received training in irregular warfare with Azov and other militias. The great risk of these foreign fighters is that they will gain combat skills and an appetite for violence, which they will carry home with them. As an American foreign fighter who travelled to Ukraine as part of Azov said, 'I came to lead a small group of volunteers from all over the West, gain some military experience and hopefully be able to send some of these guys back home to pass on their skills and their knowledge.'[290]

The Australian Security Intelligence Organisation (ASIO) has voiced concerns about Australians joining the conflict in Ukraine and linking with outfits such as Azov.[291] Australian neo-Nazis were identified as having participated in fighting in Ukraine.[292] One of them was connected to an Australian neo-Nazi group called Right Wing Resistance, whose members are responsible for burning down a church, threatening Muslims and targeting a Jewish museum.[293] However, when Australian authorities questioned the man upon his return from Ukraine, he was assessed as not being a threat.

Unlike fighters who have travelled to Syria and Iraq to fight for Islamic State, Australia is less empowered to deal with the foreign fighters who travel to Ukraine. The former Morrison government decided not to enact a recommendation from the Independent National Security Legislation Monitor that *all* foreign fighting become illegal under Australian law,[294] instead initiating a 'declared area offence'[295] only designating specific regions as no-travel zones prosecutable under Australian law. Though Australian public officials have warned people against travelling to Ukraine to participate in the war, the current legislation is unclear about the legality of Australian fighters participating in the Ukraine conflict – on either the Russian or Ukrainian side.[296]

A TRANSNATIONAL MOVEMENT

While the threat of foreign fighters committing violence back in their home countries is real, I would argue that the greater risk is a latent one[297] – the consolidation of a transnational movement networked across the globe. According to its international secretary Olena Semenyaka, Azov seeks foreign fighters and sympathisers so they can be 'potential leaders of such cells in their home countries', to 'spread ideas about creation of a new geopolitical union and promote [Azov's] political ideas to the masses'.[298] In interviews with the media, she has said, 'We think globally.'[299]

Semenyaka has made several outreach trips to Europe to meet with like-minded far-right groups and has hosted American far-right and neo-Nazi figures. Like other right-wing organisations, Semenyaka says, 'We are not resigning ourselves to the boundaries of thinking in terms of a single region. We defend not only the Ukrainian nation, national identity, but also the Slavic element, the European element, and in the end – the white race.'

Heidi Beirich, director of the Southern Poverty Law Center's Intelligence Project, says given these international connections, it is important to reconsider the nature of the threat.

We conceive of this problem as being a domestic one . . . but that's not the case. It has never been the case that these people didn't think in a global way. They may have acted in ways that looked domestic but the thinking was always about building an international movement.[300]

CHAPTER SEVEN

Extremely online

Michael (not his real name) is a former Australian fascist. He recently told ABC Radio about how he first got involved in right-wing extremism. Politically active from the age of 19, Michael became a youth leader in a minor far-right political party around the time of a heightened terrorism risk from Islamic State, rising Islamophobia and fevered debate around the role of Muslims and migrants in Australia. Michael describes how this atmosphere inspired him to become engaged with Reclaim Australia, a far-right protest movement that organised rallies to mobilise a 'public response to Islamic extremism and a protest against minority groups who want to change Australia's cultural identity'. Though they presented themselves simply as a bunch of 'concerned mums and dads',[301] there were also neo-Nazi white supremacists involved and it was at these rallies that Michael first rubbed elbows with those elements.

But, Michael explains, it was not at the rallies that he veered from the far-right into the extreme right wing. For that he needed the internet.

'I started engaging with a lot of conservative Facebook groups to see what was happening amongst a lot of those sorts of people . . . and that got me started going down the rabbit hole.' Online, he became exposed to the full gamut of right-wing extremist content, a lot of it on mainstream platforms such as Facebook and YouTube. For Michael, listening to and reading these influencers, 'they just seemed to make sense. It was like they were speaking some hidden truth that people were too afraid to talk about.'

It was not long until he encountered Great Replacement and 'white genocide' propaganda. And the content he was exposed to online became more and more extreme as he moved from mainstream platforms to closed online groups. 'It almost became like a form of desensitisation where you become more open to the edgy memes. [At first] you think, "this is going too far", [but] the more you get exposed to those sorts of things the less they seemed like they were really severe or extreme.'

Michael wasn't just exposed to extreme content online. He was being actively targeted and recruited in online spaces where this content was being posted. Soon, someone reached out to him online and asked to meet in person. From there, he became involved in the Victorian neo-Nazi group the Lads Society, now called the National Socialist Network.[302]

Former recruiters for the movement have said that they monitored far-right forums for people they thought would be open to engagement. Recruiters would track the comments sections to see 'who's really engaging with more edgy memes'. Those people would be asked to meet in person and were then initiated into more hardcore groups if they passed the vetting. They targeted younger people in particular.[303] Michael ultimately became an online extremist influencer himself. He created a Facebook page that amassed a huge following and was a 'must read' in Australian neo-Nazi circles. Eventually, he started recruiting others via closed extremist digital spaces.[304]

Michael's story demonstrates the internet's increasingly prominent role in people's involvement in extremist movements. As one academic review of the internet and extremism summarised, 'Today, the internet is no longer just one part of the spectrum of extremist activism – it has become a primary operational environment, in which political ideologies are realized, attacks planned, and social movements made.'[305] One doesn't need to travel to a conflict zone, formally sign up to an organisation or even attend a meeting to feel and be part of a network or community. Rather, individuals and groups can engage in an extremist movement through 'the connective tissue' of the internet.[306]

The rise of Islamic State awoke policymakers and the public to the use of online platforms by terrorist groups and the role of the internet in violent extremism. But while we were focusing on Islamic State, the internet was having an enormous impact on the growth and transnationalisation of the extreme right as well.

Far-right extremists were some of the earliest adopters of internet technology, recognising its huge potential as a communications and mobilisation tool.[307] Before most households even had a computer, the white supremacist movement in the United States was plugged into the early internet to spread its message and amass recruits.[308] The US-based Anti-Defamation League (ADL) reported as early as 1983 that American white supremacist groups were among the first to use dial-up bulletin board systems. Even in the early 1980s, this 'computerized hatemongering' was seen as a danger that not only facilitated the spread of 'bigotry and anti-democratic propaganda', but could have its biggest impact on 'impressionable young people' who would increasingly be using computers.[309]

The ADL report that first publicised the use of online networks by American white supremacists and neo-Nazi message boards did well to document this early adoption. However, it was less prescient in its prediction that 'although the purveyors of this hate material have clearly adapted to the "computer age", there is little to suggest that this represents a great leap forward in the spread of anti-Semitic and racist propaganda'.

Unfortunately, the modern internet has led to the exponential growth of right-wing extremist narratives, hate speech, deviant online behaviour and anti-Semitic conspiracies. It has greatly enhanced communication, interchange and ease of networking among right-wing extremists. The distinction between online and real world right-wing extremist activities is now difficult to make.

The internet has helped transform the identity and purpose of local right-wing extremist groups and individuals, facilitating the interchange between right-wing extremist strands such as anti-government movements, violent conspiratorial movements, white supremacists and other racial or ethnic supremacists.

It has allowed them to more easily connect and cross between political and ideological goals, narratives, strategies and subcultures.

For many right-wing extremists today, the internet is where they first encounter extreme ideologies and communities. Despite efforts to deplatform them, right-wing extremists are still a presence on mainstream social media platforms. Those that have been deplatformed or want a safer space to spout their hateful ideologies have migrated to alternative social media sites with little to no content moderation such as Gab and Telegram. Stormfront, the longest-running continuous white supremacist online forum, has been around since the 1990s.

COMMUNITY AND CULTURE

For individuals who become radicalised into right-wing extremism, it is not just the content that appeals, but the community that comes with it. We often underestimate the importance of communities when examining extremist movements. Many extremists just want to belong to a group. 'Communities are sort of dying in Australia,' says one former extremist. 'You used to have these big communities. You could go to the RSL [club]. But I feel like a lot of young guys have felt very isolated because so many of those communities are now online. So, they are sort of a fraternity like a brotherhood.'[310]

The feeling that communities are dying is rooted in reality. Robert Putnam's *Bowling Alone* (2000) famously outlined how the social capital that binds American communities is disintegrating. The trend has continued and is common to Western societies. We are increasingly disconnected from family, friends, neighbours, local organisations, religious institutions and our democratic structures. But the desire for community still burns, and some fulfil that need through involvement in extremist movements.

Along with community comes culture, which can be defined in many different ways, but all definitions understand it as something that brings together individuals or groups. Culture gives *shared* meaning; it is a type of mutual understanding. It is not something one can ever experience alone.

Scholar Thomas Hegghammer, who has researched jihadi culture, writes: 'militancy is about more than bombs and doctrines. It is also about rituals, customs, and dress codes. It is about music, films, and story-telling. It is about sports, jokes, and food.'[311] As jihadism developed, it became more than the sum of its parts. It was not just a collection of individuals, movements and events, but a new 'culture or subculture . . . with a potential to radicalise by transcending borders'.[312]

Similarly, right-wing extremism has evolved into a transnational subculture by encompassing shared values, spaces, myths, images, slogans, symbols, idols, aesthetics and artefacts. Examples include MMA tournaments and fight clubs, the adoption of the 'trad wife' (short for traditional wife) persona[313] by women on the far right who extol the conventional role of wife and mother in the blogs, advice columns and recipe books they create. So-called Traditionalists who philosophise against Enlightenment ideals and promote medievalism. Then there are the far-right 'prepper' groups who live off-grid and stockpile weapons and provisions for doomsday conflicts, which they actively stoke. The veganism of some neo-Nazis or the development of the online 'fasc-wave' aesthetic, which mixes 1980s synth music and new wave images. There is a militant wellness ethos permeating the far right that focuses on bodily autonomy and purity. Even fashion and the cultivation of an aesthetic – whether it is the Proud Boys' black and yellow Fred Perry polos (now withdrawn from sale), the Boogaloo Boys' Hawaiian shirts, or QAnon paraphernalia and red MAGA hats – are all part of the accumulation and manifestation of transnational right-wing extremist subculture.

THE MEME-IFICATION OF THE EXTREME RIGHT

Modern right-wing extremist expression and culture is heavily dependent on the internet for its aesthetics and tone, especially through the use of memes. Because modern right-wing extremism has developed alongside online culture writ large, it can be difficult to discern what is extremism and what is just trolling – the 'I did it for the lulz' freewheeling, chaotic nature of many online spaces. Internet culture and far-right culture often overlap. What is part of one becomes a part of the other.

Take for example websites such as 4chan, 8chan and 8kun. Chan (short for channel) sites began appearing in 2003. They were online forums for anonymous users to post anything and everything, organised into thematic threads. Then, as now, there are no accounts and no usernames, and posts expire after a certain period of time. Chan sites were foundational to the modern internet. They were 'the original incubators for a huge number of memes and behaviours that we now consider central to mainstream internet culture'.[314] Much of the content is about run of the mill topics such as pop culture, anime and cooking. Hacktivist collectives such as Anonymous started on chan sites.

But chans were 'lawless by design'.[315] The logic of the sites made them synonymous with bad behaviour and an unaccountable, ironic, nihilistic, anything-goes culture that merged all too easily with far-right ethos. Chan sites were responsible for the internet's biggest hoaxes and cyberbullying incidents, and for hosting its most abhorrent and vile content. This is especially true of 8chan's '/pol/' (politically incorrect) boards, where the most extreme content appears. In 2014, 8chan became widely known after the eruption of Gamergate, a coordinated online harassment campaign against women in computer gaming. But it soon came to be associated with a string of mass shootings by right-wing extremists in which the killers would spend copious amounts of time engaging with chan board content and its community. Chans were where they would later post their manifestos.

In 2019 alone, 8chan was directly implicated in several high-profile right-wing extremist terrorist attacks.[316] John Earnest, who shot at worshippers at a California synagogue, killing one, was enmeshed in the far-right message boards of 8chan. The El Paso shooter who killed 23 people at a Walmart store was also radicalised via 8chan. Before the attack, he posted his manifesto on the site, saying he was inspired by Brenton Tarrant's manifesto and the unmoderated discussions on 8chan that glorified his mass shooting. Philip Manshaus, who killed his stepsister before going on to shoot up a mosque in Norway in 2019, was also inspired by Tarrant and was a frequent user of chan sites, where he admitted his extremist views were formed.[317]

The use of memes[318] is common to both far-right and online cultures, with so many of the memes originating on chan sites. A regular internet user can send a meme of LOLcats, Futurama Fry or Distracted Boyfriend with no hidden agenda. However, extremists use memes such as Pepe the Frog, The Doge or Wojak to communicate all sorts of ideas – from condescension of liberals and political correctness to the denigration of marginalised communities and minorities, or criticism of 'normies', the mainstream who unquestioningly live their lives.

Memes are a clever way to communicate and increase receptiveness to extremist ideas, identify the like-minded and even spur violence, all under the guise of plausible deniability. Memes are successful at engaging people in extremist content because it is difficult to discern intent online – posts could be facetious or serious, or both.[319] This ambiguity is a fundamental aspect of online culture and one that helps spread extremist views. Known as Poe's law, the concept is that without a clear indicator of a poster's intent, a parody of an extreme view can be misinterpreted as a sincere expression of that very position. The OK hand gesture is a Platonic ideal of this ambiguity. It is possibly one of the most anodyne gestures one could make. How it turned into a white power symbol is an interesting case study of Poe's law.

The OK sign was first presented as a parody of a white supremacist gesture. In 2015, an internet user named Pizza Party Ben made a Vine (short-form video) of himself making the gesture, captioning it 'White guys be like'. Far-right online users started spreading the video as a hoax – claiming that the shape of his hand spelled out the letters WP (white power) – to trick people into thinking it was a new white supremacist signal. The OK sign meme started as a 'shitpost' directed at the political correctness brigade who are willing to believe that anything can be a hate symbol and were sure to overreact.[320]

Then, far-right internet influencers and Trump supporters started using it too, probably in this ironic spirit, but . . . maybe sometimes not. Then *actual* white supremacists started using it. In 2019, Brenton Tarrant flashed the OK sign in a courtroom appearance. After that, organisations that track extremist symbols were compelled to officially list it as a hate symbol and it became an authentic marker of white supremacist and other far-right ideologies.[321] The OK sign is an example of 'Trojan Horse' hate. It was 'actual bigotry camouflaged as ironic bigotry'. But it blunted the ability of normies to distinguish between the two, thus weaponising sincerity and gullibility.[322]

Jenny Morrison, wife of former Australian prime minister Scott Morrison, was accused in 2021 of using the sign as a white power symbol. Following reporting that a close friend of Mrs Morrison was running a prolific online account that spread QAnon content, people began scrutinising photos of her for the sign. That the spouse of an Australian prime minister was suspected of secretly harbouring white supremacist views whipped up political opponents on the left. On one hand, Morrison's accusers appeared unhinged for making the accusation as there was no evidence that she espoused such views. But the accusation simultaneously planted a seed of doubt about Morrison's extremist associations. The episode was an exquisite manifestation of Poe's law and the intentions of far-right online trolls.

Participating in trolling, shitposting and subversive dark humour serves another purpose. It fosters belonging among online extremist communities.[323] Transgressive, supposedly edgy humour strengthens collective identity and bonds between anonymous and atomised online actors. They are all in on the joke while the rest of us are left offended or wondering if they are serious.

Humour offers a very effective way to increase the acceptability of extremist positions, normalising violence and dehumanising others through subversive irony.[324] Humour can also provide plausible deniability for extreme views. Take for example the leaked 'style guide' of white supremacist website *The Daily Stormer*. In addition to formatting guidelines, it dictates:

> Generally, when using racial slurs, it should come across as half-joking – like a racist joke everyone laughs at because it's true. This follows the generally light tone of the site. It should not come across as genuinely raging vitriol. That is a turn-off . . . The indoctrinated should not be able to tell if we are joking or not.[325]

The style guide's author admits though that 'this is obviously a ploy and I actually do want to [kill Jews]'. He also advises that contributors read Adolf Hitler's *Mein Kampf* and that in every post they should 'blame the Jews for everything'.[326] In case it wasn't absolutely clear, the guide continues: 'There should be a conscious agenda to dehumanise the enemy, to the point where people are ready to laugh at their deaths. So it isn't clear that we are doing this – as that would be a turn-off to most normal people – we rely on lulz.'[327]

Trolling, creating 'dank memes' and engaging in extremist and abusive discourse online is a problem in and of itself. But often, it does not just stay online. The Christchurch massacre had a deeply disturbing online/offline convergence. The manifesto that Brenton Tarrant posted before his shooting spree is both an artefact of this culture and draws heavily *from* online culture. The entire document referred liberally to memes and in-jokes that only the extremely online radical subculture would understand and appreciate. It also incited others to create memes in the aftermath of the attack. Tarrant livestreamed his massacre with the goal of 'making the act itself a meme'.[328] And although his act of terrorism grew out of extremist shitposting culture, Tarrant wrote in his manifesto that 'it's time to stop shitposting and time to make a real life effort'.[329]

THE NOT-SO-LONE ATTACKER

When we think of right-wing extremist violence, probably the first thing that comes to mind is a white, male mass shooter. This is unsurprising given that much far-right discourse is about white, Western masculinity under threat. Examples range from Anders Breivik to Brenton Tarrant to Dylann Roof, who killed nine African American worshippers in a church in South Carolina in 2015. Robert

Bowers shot dead 11 people at the Tree of Life synagogue in Pennsylvania in 2018. Stephan Balliet attacked a synagogue in Halle, Germany in 2019. Then there is Patrick Crusius, the 2019 El Paso mass shooter, and most recently Payton Gendron, who killed ten people at a grocery store in an African American neighbourhood in Buffalo, New York in May 2022.

We have called them 'lone wolves' because they are often socially isolated, acting of their own volition and seemingly unconnected to any broader movement. But while these attackers may appear to have emerged *sui generis*, they have actually risen out of right-wing extremist online cultures and communities.[330] The digital spaces where these individuals lurk are not just a collection of individual entities, but have become, as one author puts it, a 'kind of many-headed trickster-god; a psychotic consciousness in its own right'.[331] Their lone action belies their interconnectedness to a broader movement facilitated via the internet, making it more difficult to distinguish between individual action and networked provocation.[332]

Brenton Tarrant was deeply enmeshed in these digital worlds. The Christchurch Royal Commission report details just how much:

He was . . . an avid internet user and online gamer. He had few childhood friends . . . . his relationships with others have been limited and superficial . . . . his limited personal engagement with others left considerable scope for influence from extreme right-wing material, which he found on the internet . . . . As a child he had unsupervised access to the internet from a computer in his bedroom. He spent much of his free time at school accessing the internet on school computers. In 2017, he told his mother that he had started using the 4chan internet message board when he was 14 years old . . . [As he got older] We have no doubt that he visited right-wing internet forums, subscribed to right-wing channels on YouTube and read a great deal about immigration, far-right political theories and historical struggles between Christianity and Islam . . . he also posted some right-wing and threatening comments.[333]

Tarrant wrote in his manifesto that his attack in Christchurch was prompted by the supposedly malevolent influence of immigration that he had seen on his travels, but the Royal Commission dismisses his account. '[O]f far more materiality was the individual's immersion during this period in the literature, and probably the online forums, of the far-right . . . we do not accept the individual's account of when and why he decided to engage in terrorism – an account that we see as propaganda.'[334]

We can also see how individual lone attacks build upon each other. An analysis of 15 right-wing extremist mass shootings between 2011 and 2019 found that the perpetrators either corresponded directly online with other attackers, referenced and praised previous attackers in online postings, studied or copied their tactics or directly stated that they drew inspiration from previous lone actor violence.[335] Lone attackers often used manifestos to connect their actions to those of others, portraying themselves as part of a chain reaction where one attack encourages and inspires another.[336] Extremism scholar J. M. Berger writes: 'the manifesto became a baton in the relay race of extremism'.[337]

These manifestos are ubiquitous online and are even translated into multiple languages.[338] Tarrant's attack became a key reference for many lone attackers, just as Tarrant had been inspired by Breivik and Roof.[339] Manshaus claimed to be a 'disciple' of Tarrant, and was inspired by Earnest and Crusius. He urged others to join this continuum: 'if you're reading this you have been elected by me,' he posted.[340]

Some lone attackers, however, are regarded with disdain or mockery by their own online communities for having a 'low score'. In other words, they are ridiculed and shamed because they did not kill enough people.[341]

The concept of low and high scores is a direct reference to kill counts in video games and points to 'gamification', a growing feature of right-wing extremism.[342] Interlinked with the use of humour and irony, it has made killing and other abhorrent actions akin to a game. And if it is just a game, it lowers the threshold for participation in violence and facilitates the radicalisation process.

An estimated 3.2 billion people worldwide play video games. Clearly, not all of them become mass shooters, so exposure to gaming alone does not lead to radicalisation. But studies have found that video games, in combination with other factors, can have an influence on a player's perception of violence. The interactive nature of games and their ability to fulfil psychological needs of competency and social connection can facilitate the online radicalisation process.[343] If you are a 'player' instead of a person – collecting points, upping your ranking to get on a leader board – you see your potential victims not as humans but as avatars or points to score and it becomes easier and even fun to kill.[344]

Online supporters of real life mass shooters do not speak of deadly violence. Instead, they refer to 'scores'. Tarrant and Breivik are acclaimed for having the highest scores, while one 8chan user posted after Crusius' attack, 'The new guy deserves some praise, he reached almost a third of the high score.'[345]

The livestreaming of the Christchurch massacre and the copycat attacks in El Paso, Halle and Buffalo also borrow from video game culture. The Christchurch Royal Commission report detailed how Tarrant was enmeshed in online role-playing and first-person shooter games and how the live streaming of his attack recalled popular shooter games such as *Call of Duty.*

THE POST-HIERARCHICAL EXTREME RIGHT

The internet has also changed the organisational principles and structure of right-wing extremism, creating a kind of 'post-organisational' and 'post-hierarchal' environment where leaders or organisations are not dictating strategy and action. Instead, individuals or cells mobilise independently, believing themselves to be connected to a wider movement and acting on behalf of a shared cause.

In fact, leaderless resistance is an established right-wing extremist strategy and is intertwined with the early history of right-wing extremist use of the internet.[346] In 1978, white nationalist William Pierce wrote a racist dystopian novel called *The Turner Diaries,* a book that has had a profound influence on the extreme right, serving as both a call to action and a guidebook for violent plotting.[347]

The book depicts a violent revolution in which a number of small cells carry out insurgent attacks that lead to the overthrow of the US government and the extermination of Jews and racial minorities, first in the United States and then the rest of the world.[348] The book is harder to find these days – Amazon only recently took it off their virtual shelves – but it remains required reading for extremists, with references to the book's plot and themes finding new life on the internet.[349] The novel has been linked to at least nine lone attackers, dozens of hate crimes and at least one attack per year since 2013.[350]

In the 1980s, US neo-Nazi James Mason published a series of newsletters called *Siege*, which explicitly advocated for a 'leaderless resistance' strategy. He called for individuals to take actions outside organisational hierarchies or chains of command as part of a move towards accelerationism – a theory of creative destruction that proposes any point of upheaval as an opportunity to accelerate the demise of current societal structures and governments, and impose new ones. This leaderless resistance strategy has been adopted particularly by neo-Nazi groups.[351]

Another influential US white nationalist and former Klansman, Louis Beam, also encouraged self-directed terrorism. In the 1980s, he published a 3400-word essay entitled – what else – *Leaderless Resistance*, explaining the strategy in the white supremacist magazine he started called *The Seditionist*. He argued that because command-and-control type organisations are prone to government infiltration and destruction, 'it will become necessary to consider other methods of organization – or as the case may very well call for: non-organization'.[352]

The leaderless resistance strategy has been the de facto operating principle of neo-Nazi and white supremacist movements ever since. Adherence to the strategy is one way right-wing extremists have been able to fly under the counter-terrorism radar and subvert any political will to label them as terrorists. As Mason wrote in an issue of *Siege*, 'The lone wolf cannot be detected, cannot be prevented, and seldom can be traced . . . [but] his greatest concern must be to pick his target well so that his act may speak so clearly for itself that no member of White America can mistake its message.'[353]

Beam, in particular, understood early the power of the internet to disseminate the idea of leaderless resistance. It would lead him in 1984 to found the online bulletin board *Liberty Net*, on which he would later republish his tract on the theory. But it was not until the internet, and specifically social networking, became more widely used that leaderless resistance was able to reach its full potential.

CHAPTER EIGHT

Covid and right-wing extremist contagion

During the height of the Covid-19 pandemic, isolated in our homes, unmoored from routines and rituals, we all spent copious amounts of time online. Pandemic restrictions limited the social interactions and relationships that regulate us. People were desperate for community and searching for answers.

The pandemic produced a collective stress and trauma that made more people susceptible to the disinformation, conspiracies and extremist narratives circulating online that offered easy and uncomplicated answers to the chaos around us.[354] Engagement with online conspiracies, disinformation and hate speech all increased during the pandemic.[355] So too did engagement in right-wing extremist forums and online spaces.

The Covid pandemic highlighted how times of crisis are ripe for conspiracists and extremists[356] and how crisis can be instrumentalised by extremist actors. Emergencies and disasters tend to expose cracks in societies. Even when the government and emergency management response has been robust, extremist actors are adept at reframing disasters and emergencies to: (1) contest government legitimacy, (2) identify groups to blame, and (3) encourage mobilisation – and in so doing tacitly incite violence – against outsider groups.

With governments granting themselves broad powers and imposing states of emergency, the Covid pandemic was the first time that many people living in democracies truly felt the heavy hand of the state. While most accepted social distancing requirements and restrictions on freedom of assembly as a necessary hardship to preserve public health, others bristled against the restrictions and considered them government overreach. The extensions of government authority and curtailing of individual liberties during the pandemic were framed by extremists as tools of social control and evidence of authoritarian tendencies, playing into a concern that temporary restrictions would become permanent.

Government restrictions, while necessary in many cases, also contributed to social and economic ills.

People lost livelihoods and loved ones without being able to properly mourn. Many blamed the state for these tragedies, which increased their susceptibility to the disinformation and conspiracy theories being spread by right-wing extremists that the public health measures were part of a broader, nefarious plot by governments to control and manipulate us. Vaccine mandates and restrictions on freedom of movement to curb the spread of the virus fed into right-wing extremist narratives about governments imposing authoritarian controls over citizens. These narratives are particularly likely to take root after a prolonged state of emergency among those feeling disempowered or with a conspiratorial mind-set.

In Australia, there was a sharp uptick in sovereign citizen and anti-government sentiment and protest spurred by those chafing against Covid restrictions and lockdowns. The lockdown measures in Victoria were among the strictest in the world.[357] The state was beset by a number of violent rallies during 2021, with some protesters displaying nooses in front of parliament. In September of that year, when the state government imposed an industry-wide shutdown and vaccine mandate for construction workers, there was a massive street protest during which the head office of the Construction, Forestry, Maritime, Mining and Energy Union (CFMEU) was attacked, with protesters later desecrating the Shrine of Remembrance. It appeared that a coordinated far-right, anti-government, anti-vax, anti-lockdown action had merged with a protest by disgruntled union members. Also during Victoria's lockdown, a man was charged with sending death threats to Victorian Premier Daniel Andrews over his government's pandemic response.[358]

During the pandemic, the sovereign citizen movement intersected with the anti-lockdown and anti-vax movements, which were turbo-charged when vaccine mandates were introduced. The three movements made common cause. The anti-lockdown movement evangelised via social media, rallying around objections to state of emergency restrictions, framing them as 'illegal', illegitimate and part of a hidden agenda by a tyrannical government. This message resonated with the sovereign citizen movement, which held similar, if not more esoteric, anti-government beliefs. Sovereign citizens believe that the government is a corporation and that individuals are not subject to government regulations because they as 'natural beings' can choose when and where to enter into a 'contract' with government. The anti-lockdown and sovereign citizen movements also attracted and interacted with a number of far-right and extremist elements that sought to find common cause and recruit among the sovereign citizen, anti-vax and anti-lockdown cohort.

The sovereign citizen/anti-lockdown movement initially coalesced and expanded via Facebook pages and groups organised to oppose state lockdowns. Through those pages, they were exposed to conspiracy theories claiming the virus was a hoax and an undercover means of expanding control. Sovereign citizens and anti-lockdown protesters would often film themselves defying lockdown restrictions and confronting authorities, later posting their videos on social media. They also used social media to spread conspiracy theories and disinformation about the pandemic, vaccinations and government regulations. Much of this disinformation was QAnon or Q-adjacent content.[359]

THE CONVOY

The quad of anti-lockdown, anti-vax, sovereign citizen and far-right movements were not confined to protest action in Melbourne. They organised in all of Australia's major cities, culminating in the February 2022 'Convoy to Canberra'. Thousands of protesters from all over the country organised via social media and Telegram, converged in the capital, setting up tents near Parliament House and the

National Library, and an 'Occupy Canberra' camp near Old Parliament House.

They harassed law enforcement and average citizens. Some appointed themselves as 'sheriffs' and attempted to issue arrest warrants for politicians.[360] One of the main organisers of the protest was arrested after police found a shotgun and ammunition in his truck.[361] It all echoed an earlier plot, disrupted by the Australian Federal Police (AFP), by a handful of people who planned to impersonate AFP officers, make arrests of politicians, and 'overthrow' the government. They circulated a fake video falsely depicting AFP Commissioner Reece Kershaw discussing plans for this supposed overthrow.[362]

Convoy to Canberra protesters also attempted to appropriate the Aboriginal Tent Embassy to push for a different kind of sovereignty agenda. When conducting an unauthorised smoking ceremony, they set fire to Old Parliament House. It was part of a broader effort by sovereign citizen movements to appropriate Aboriginal sovereignty efforts.[363] Through this 'blackfishing' (when far-right groups attempt to claim Black support) they are co-opting a longstanding Indigenous movement to attract credibility and legitimacy. This effort is accompanied by a campaign of disinformation claiming that Indigenous communities in the Northern Territory are being forcibly vaccinated and 'murdered' by 'bioweapons'.[364]

The Canberra protests were inspired by the Canadian truckers' 'Freedom Convoy', also a response to vaccine mandates but broadened to include far-right and QAnon figures with an anti-government agenda. QAnon symbols and swastikas were visible at the protests.[365] Key organisers of the protest called for the toppling of the Canadian government. Four protesters were charged with conspiracy to murder police in response to plans to violently disrupt police efforts to break the blockade.[366]

The Canadian actions inspired similar anti-government protests and calls for revolution, not only in Australia but globally – in France, New Zealand, Belgium and elsewhere. Far-right figures around the world, including in Australia, praised and amplified the Canadian protests online. Some have called for similar demonstrations in their countries, including far-right Australian politicians such as George Christensen.[367]

In Australia, as restrictions eased and Convoy to Canberra protesters dissipated, they transitioned towards consolidating into a political movement. The Reignite Democracy Australia party, which formed on the back of anti-government opposition during the pandemic, contested seats in the 2022 federal election and found common cause with other far-right Australian parties such as the United Australia Party and One Nation.[368] Similarly in Canada, right-wing politicians are eager to pick up support from the convoy constituency.[369]

In the United States, Covid restrictions generated even more vehement opposition. In 2020, for example, the FBI disrupted the plotted kidnapping of Michigan's governor by extremists motivated by her enacting state-wide coronavirus restrictions.[370] In April 2022, a man deliberately derailed a train into a US Navy hospital ship docked nearby, claiming the ship's presence in Los Angeles was part of a government takeover.[371] Head of the US coronavirus taskforce Dr Anthony Fauci has needed extra security due to the number of credible threats to his safety.[372] And FBI agents killed right-wing extremist Timothy Wilson in a shootout following his plan to use a car bomb to blow up a hospital treating Covid patients.[373]

In a leaked 2020 memo, the US Department of Homeland Security said that white supremacists and neo-Nazis were obliging any infected members to spread the virus to law enforcement and minority communities.[374] Groups that track right-wing extremism, such as the Anti-Defamation League, have identified memes on right-wing forums including 'What to Do if You Get Corona 19', which instruct readers to 'visit your local mosque, visit your local synagogue, spend the day on public transport, spend time in your local diverse neighborhood'.[375]

The pandemic has played into anti-globalisation and nativist attitudes among extremists. Data extracted from Australian far-right and extremist social media has shown persistent narratives about white supremacy, the failure of multiculturalism, the contribution of globalisation to the spread of Covid, and the opportunity presented by pandemic restrictions to press for permanent limits to immigration.[376]

White supremacist groups have blamed multiculturalism for the pandemic and ethnic diversity for the spread of the virus – calling it the 'diversity flu'. The United Nations has highlighted a growth in 'Covid-19 related hate speech' that targets certain ethnic groups or foreigners, warning that it could 'trigger social unrest and intergroup violence, possibly enhancing the conditions conducive to conflict and atrocity crimes'.[377]

Right-wing extremists see disasters and emergencies as an opportunity to challenge government legitimacy and spread disinformation and conspiracy theories to sow distrust and foment polarisation. They have latched onto emergencies as catalysts for the 'accelerationism' promoted by groups such as Atomwaffen Division, The Base and Sonnenkrieg Division.[378] The Boogaloo movement in the United States has also been a proponent of this theory – their name a reference to what its adherents believe to be a future civil war. Some elements of US-based Proud Boys chapters have also integrated into accelerationist movements.[379] In Australia, far-right movements including the National Socialist Network have promoted accelerationism during the Covid pandemic. For accelerationists, a crisis presents a perfect opportunity.

The adoption of accelerationism by violent extremists is problematic for disaster management and broader efforts to counter violent extremism because it implies that any crisis will be an opportunity for violence, regardless of a government's emergency response. Therefore, government responses must include a recognition that these crises will play into the hands of those who want to stoke division and exploit the conditions to promote conflict and undermine social cohesion.

CHAPTER NINE

The fringe majority: right-wing extremism and the threat to democracy

Though this book is an examination of extremism, many elements of right-wing extremism are no longer confined to the fringe – they have gone mainstream. This is evident in the widespread belief in right-wing adjacent QAnon conspiracy theories, the mainstreaming of xenophobic and Islamophobic sentiment, the persistence of Trumpism in the United States and the veering to the far right by traditionally conservative parties.

Right-wing extremists are no longer hiding under hoods and robes. They are not just neo-Nazis menacing the streets in combat boots and leather. Instead, right-wing extremists come from the very centre of our democratic societies. As one former extremist explained:

No one wore hoods, they wore slacks . . . They were EMTs [emergency medical technicians], they were lawyers, they were doctors, they were your neighbours, they were your family members still believing in all of this stuff. This is what makes all of this so dangerous. You can't spot the [extremist] anymore.[380]

This mainstream turn is motivated by many of the structural factors discussed in earlier chapters. But to better understand how right-wing extremism has seeped into the mainstream, one must examine the role of two pillars of society: media and politics.

MEDIA MAINSTREAMING

For far-right extremists to effectively communicate their goals and objectives, they cannot just depend on their own social media or clandestine organising. Extremism, particularly terrorism, is a performative and communicative act. It needs a broad audience, and for that, extremists need the media. For what extremists want most is to influence and be taken seriously by the mainstream.

One cannot talk about the Fourth Estate as a monolith. Journalism that is objective and free from influence is critical to the functioning of a healthy democracy. Journalists hold the powerful to account and shed light on important issues and stories in the public interest. Many journalists and media outlets have played critical roles in investigating and exposing right-wing extremist movements and actors. In addition to my own research work, my understanding and analysis of these movements is indebted to journalists' reporting.

But there is a strain of illiteracy among many journalists when it comes to far-right extremism and how it uses the media. There has also been a negligence in some segments of the media when covering issues that right-wing extremist movements and radical right political movements capitalise on, particularly around race, gender, LGBTQI rights and immigration. More egregiously, far-right and extreme-right influencers have been platformed by influential media outlets.[381] In Australia, for example, Sky News has featured known right-wing extremist influencer and neo-Nazi Blair Cottrell[382] as well as Lauren Southern.[383]

But this type of coverage is by no means confined to Murdoch-owned media outlets. Even the flagship ABC News program *Four Corners* has featured right-wing extremists such as Steve Bannon, a former Trump adviser and chairman of Breitbart News (a far-right website known for spouting racist and conspiratorial content, which had called for the 'beheading' of Dr Anthony Fauci and other government officials during the pandemic), and Henry 'Enrique' Tarrio, one-time leader of the Proud Boys. While the producers of the program argued that people like Bannon were influential and worthy of coverage and that ignoring them would not make their views go away,[384] there is an underappreciated risk to giving airtime to such individuals, even if they are covered critically.

In platforming these right-wing figures, mainstream media outlets have given extremists a key opportunity to shift the 'Overton window' – the spectrum of ideas the public is willing to accept at a given time. According to Macquarie University researchers Julian Droogan and Lise Waldek, who examine this phenomenon in their research of the Australian far-right, these mainstream spaces allow extremists to frame their movements and positions as 'expressing beliefs through appeals to critical thinking [and] a rejection of political correctness'.[385] In so doing, they push against the limits of acceptable discourse and policies and create space for far-right ideas to enter into the mainstream.[386]

Media coverage of the issues that right-wing extremists care about amplifies its messaging and mobilisation. Without constant vigilance and wise editorial decisions, it is surprisingly easy for mainstream news publications to be 'commandeered as unwitting mouthpieces for extremism'.[387]

A research team from Victoria University found that some of the most shared online posts among Australian right-wing extremists were news reports by mainstream outlets. It revealed how extremists are emboldened by news coverage and commentary that they believe lends credibility to their cause.[388] Professor Debra Smith, who was part of the research team, said mainstream media coverage around immigration, Islam, race, crime and other political and social issues of the day 'gives [far-right groups] a certain sense that their ideas are legitimate. They point to issues in the press to show that they are not outsiders, that they are not extreme.'[389] Right-wing extremists capitalise on mainstream media coverage of core right-wing extremist themes by saying that their positions are just part of the 'respectable debate'.

Discussions and commentary around migration in the mainstream media in Australia have amplified far-right talking points and positions. Before the emergence of the Identitarian movement and mass casualty attacks motivated by the Great Replacement Theory, mainstream right-leaning media figures and commentators with large audiences framed immigrants as threats. While these media figures did not advocate violence, they nevertheless added to the background noise and often framed the immigration debate in ways that played into people's anxieties and resentments, which extremists could then exploit.

To take an example, Andrew Bolt, a major Australian media figure with his own television program and nationally syndicated newspaper column, wrote about the threat of a 'tidal wave of immigrants' that had 'swept away what is left of our national identity . . . not just crowding our cities but changing our culture'.[390] Bolt and other commentators are within their rights to hold these views. But in espousing them in such a public way and on such a broad platform, the narratives play into the hands of extremist movements who can point to these voices, acclimatising the public to more extreme positions.

Often the media's coverage of extremist actors and movements leads to amplification of extremist positions, allowing them to more readily enter mainstream consciousness. By reporting on every extremist controversy, outrage or repugnant action, many media outlets contribute to the spread of these ideas, even if it is not their intention.[391] Right-wing extremists strive for this kind of attention. According to a comprehensive review of research evidence, far-right movements 'exert disproportionate agenda setting power [when] they manage to attract high media attention'.[392]

At the same time, many media outlets and journalists benefit from coverage of far-right actors and movements.[393] At no time was this more apparent than in the coverage of Donald Trump. Much attention has been focused on the role of media outlets such as Fox News in the rise of Trump, but not enough on how the media landscape *as a whole* contributed.

While Trump railed against the 'lamestream media' and 'fake news', and sought to undermine the public's trust in journalism, he was also responsible for massive ratings rises for cable news channels and in the subscription levels of major publications around the world, especially those he criticised most. He raised the profiles and made the careers of many journalists who covered him.

Despite the damage Trump did by fomenting distrust in the media, outlets continued to cover him and his outrageous behaviour. Even when they did cover Trump objectively, the media tended to 'merchandise anxiety' around his presidency. They provided Trump with the necessary oxygen to fuel his campaign.[394] And he obliged by providing more outrage for the media to cover, creating a cycle of mutual dependency.

This dynamic did not exist only between Trump and far-right leaning media outlets such as Fox News and its host Tucker Carlson, who at times privately advised Trump.[395] It also existed among other news outlets such as *The New York Times* and CNN. Head of CNN at the time, Jeff Zucker, played a major role in raising Trump's profile, having executive produced Trump's reality show *The Apprentice* at another network, and later giving Trump overwhelming coverage in the crowded field of Republican primary candidates in 2016, even broadcasting his rallies in their entirety.[396] In later years, when CNN coverage was largely critical or considered 'anti-Trump', the network continued to cover him, and their ratings continued to increase.[397]

The incessant critical coverage of Trump fed into the outrage and polarisation that nourishes extremism. Zucker himself, reflecting on the relationship between the network and Trump, said, 'Not calling [Trump's behaviour] out more for what it was, and then holding the other side more accountable, that was probably a mistake.'[398]

The pattern was repeated in the Australian media, with Trump becoming part of the daily news cycle. But it was not just about Trump. The same dynamic was at play when the media covered the supposed 'African gangs crisis', gender issues and LGBTQI or immigration policies – inflaming hot button issues through incessant, uncritical coverage because it increased clicks and brought eyes to the page.

MAINSTREAMING POLITICS

Healthy liberal democracies tend to weed out or marginalise extremist elements. Adherence to democratic values such as pluralism, liberty, equality and justice carve off extreme views and policies. But conviction in these values is waning for all the reasons discussed in earlier chapters. The electorate is increasingly disillusioned with mainstream politics and the elites who run it. According to academic Mark Triffett, 'As mainstream voters turn off or tune out, democracy's inherent barriers against extremism are dismantled as well. This leaves democracy hollowed out and at risk of being hijacked by those at the fringes.'[399] And at the mercy of populist far-right figures.

In 2019, Indian Prime Minister Narendra Modi made an official visit to the United States. It was a moment that crystallised for me the very real threat that far-right populists pose to democracy. Though the media coverage of the visit focused mostly on energy partnerships, trade deals and the visibility of America's large Indian diaspora, I couldn't help but watch Trump's appearance at a 'Howdy Modi!' rally and think: here were the leaders of the two brightest stars in the firmament of global democracy, led by men with ties to extremist movements and actors who have incited violence, targeted minorities via legislation and eroded their multicultural democracies. The leader of the oldest democracy in the world, the United States, and the leader of the largest democracy, India – both multicultural, pluralistic and officially secular nations – were led by radical right leaders.

Modi and Trump, along with Brazil's Bolsonaro and Hungary's Orbán are leaders who have risen to prominence though electoral democracy but who are themselves threats to liberal democracy. These radical right populists are appropriating the appeals of the far right and extreme right and in so doing are eroding democracy from within.

Right-wing extremist movements are defined by their rejection of electoral democracy in favour of revolutionary violence, but there is no doubt that they are connected to far-right strands that *do* participate in politics. Right-wing extremist ideas are mainstreamed through leaders who espouse what political scientist Cas Mudde terms 'radical right populism'. These radical right populists and far-right politicians, who claim to reject the elite but who are actually part of an *alternative* elite, are riding on the coattails of many of the ideas of right-wing extremist movements.

These far-right politicians advocate for nativism and promote authoritarianism. They do not advocate for *all* of the people, only *their* people. They undermine social cohesion and foment polarisation by framing the other side of the nation as the enemy. And they promote a sense that anyone who is not of their movement – the opposition political party, government officials and public servants upholding the institutions of democracy – as illegitimate.

Like extremist movements, radical right populists use disinformation and conspiracies to undermine democratic government and institutions through what the late, great political scientist Ehud Sprinzak termed 'transformational delegitimation'.[400] This theory argues that conspiracies and disinformation gradually and systematically create a crisis of confidence in the political leadership, which leads to a loss of confidence in the political system, which finally dehumanises individuals and justifies violent targeting of those who perpetuate the political system.

Like right-wing extremists, these far-right populists use conspiracy theories and disinformation to perpetuate the idea that government institutions have no use or value or are the hostile actors, not legitimate authorities. Once something or someone is determined to be illegitimate, anything is justified to get rid of them – including violence and subversion of the democratic process.

THE TRUMP FACTOR

The mainstreaming of right-wing extremism via far-right populism both precedes and extends beyond Donald Trump. Yet, it is difficult to overstate how much the election of Trump has contributed to the growth and mainstreaming of modern right-wing extremism, not just in the United States, but globally. Trump's trajectory and that of his supporters – from rogue candidate to president who incited violent insurrection to overturn the results of an election – reveals a lot about how right-wing extremism has gone mainstream and threatens liberal democracy. One cannot talk about right-wing extremism's threat to democracy without examining Trump. From the moment he descended the golden escalator at Trump Towers to launch his presidential campaign in 2015, he has tried to take democracy down with him.

Trump was elected because of, not despite, the fact that some things he said directly reflected the concerns of right-wing extremists. Through the 'Make America Great Again' slogan that he borrowed from Ronald Reagan,[401] Trump harkened back to an idealised past to which right-wing extremists also cling. The Trump administration's trade policy and tough stance on China tapped into anti-globalisation sentiment and grievances about the stagnation of wages and displaced job opportunities. It also legitimised negative views of minorities.[402] Trump's attacks on fellow billionaire George Soros, accusing him of funding a caravan of migrants to steal jobs and votes, was a repetition of right-wing extremist conspiracies about the New World Order and mirrored their targeting of Jews. Right-wing extremists cheered when Trump vowed to stop the supposed flood of murderous illegal immigrants into the United States.

And even though Trump himself is part of the 'one percent' – a businessman billionaire from New York who became rich via his father's legacy – he did not have to reach far from his roots as a boy from Queens who never quite made it in the upper echelons of Manhattan society to construct his anti-establishment persona. While horrifying Americans on both seaboards and many of the country's global allies, Trump was enormously appealing precisely *because* he was crude and rude, making him a superb troll of the liberal left elite while muscling out the conservative right-wing establishment, both avowed enemies of the extreme right.

Not all right-wing extremists supported Trump or necessarily viewed him as part of their cause. Many could not stomach his personal and familial connections to Judaism. Nevertheless, his election provided enormous legitimacy and succour to these movements.

Trump has done a great deal to mainstream white supremacist and fascist positions, not just through dog whistling, but by actually saying the quiet parts out loud. He has repeated their slogans and talking points, retweeted their memes, excused them when they committed violence and incited them to violence himself. His election was proof to many right-wing extremists that their views and positions are not only correct but supported within the mainstream; that while they are the vanguard, there is a silent majority that agrees with their positions.

Right-wing extremist communities paid close attention to Trump's statements and social media feed, looking for hints and celebrating their influence. As tech reporter Kevin Roose of *The New York Times* wrote in a piece examining the interplay of Trump and online far-right communities, 'when they find those clues, [like Trump repeating or retweeting something extremists posted online] they take them as evidence that Mr Trump is "/ourguy/", a label for people internet extremists believe share their views, but who are unable to say so directly in public.'[403]

American neo-Nazi leader James Mason said, 'I am not ashamed to say that I shed a tear of joy at [Trump's] win.'[404] Mason believed Trump was a proof of concept, that given time and driven by accelerationist pressures, a majority of Americans would tip the scales in their favour.[405] Trump's popularity and promises to 'drain the swamp' also indicated to neo-Nazis that the average citizen may be now more amenable to authoritarian governance and had given up on liberalism.

There is debate about whether Trump was himself an active supporter, rather than just an enabler, of right-wing extremists. During the opening debate of the 2020 presidential campaign, when moderator Chris Wallace asked Trump bluntly whether he would condemn white supremacist violence, Trump at first equivocated, but then this exchange happened:

'You want to call them . . . What do you want to call them? Give me a name,' Trump asked Wallace.

Wallace tried to clarify: 'White supremacists and, white supremacists and right-wing . . .'.

Biden then interjected by saying, 'The Proud Boys.'

'Proud Boys, stand back and stand by,' Trump propositioned. 'I'll tell you what, I'll tell you what, somebody's got to do something about antifa and the left, because this is not a right-wing problem. This is a left-wing problem.'

The 'something' was left unsaid but well understood. After years of innuendo, Trump not only appealed to extremist organisations to vote for him and to signal that he shared their views, but he essentially gave the green light – live on national television – for white supremacist groups and right-wing armed groups to stand at the ready to commit violence on his behalf.[406] In the same debate, when asked whether he would urge his supporters to refrain from civil unrest on election day, Trump said, 'I'm urging my supporters to go into the polls and watch very carefully . . . bad things happen.'[407]

As Trump's first term neared its end and the prospect of his re-election became more distant, his incitement of violence grew. Just a few weeks after the presidential debate, he again stoked armed protests in Michigan against the state capitol, tweeting 'Free Michigan', claiming that the Second Amendment – the right to keep and bear arms – was under siege. A few of these armed protesters were ultimately arrested on terrorism charges for a plot to kidnap Michigan governor Gretchen Whitmer over the state's Covid shutdown.

The storming of state capitols by right-wing extremists in America was a preview of what was to come. Analysis of the participants in the siege of the US Capitol building in Washington, DC on 6 January 2021 shows that they were made up of large numbers of individuals with ties to known right-wing extremist groups, white supremacists and right-wing militias in the United States.[408] Michael Jensen, a researcher with the University of Maryland's domestic radicalisation project, analysed 244 defendants arrested during the Capitol siege. He found that 30 per cent had known ties to extremist movements. Extremist groups and militias such as the Three Percenters, the Oath Keepers and the Proud Boys had advance plans of the storming of the Capitol. Stewart Rhodes, the founder of the Oath Keepers, had broadcast for weeks before the election that he was ready to take orders from Trump to engage in violence and that they were preparing for the next civil war. On far-right conspiracy theorist Alex Jones' InfoWars podcast, Rhodes said he had 'good men on the ground already'.[409] The House Select Committee investigating the insurrection is examining the coordination between the Trump administration, Republican lawmakers and these extremist groups during the storming of the Capitol.[410] So far, they have presented a damning case.

A few extremists have used the 'Trump made me do it' defence when their actions landed them in court. White supremacist leader Matthew Heimbach, who was on trial for assaulting a Black woman at a Trump rally, filed a countersuit saying that if he was found liable for damages because he 'acted pursuant to the directives and requests of Donald J. Trump and Donald J. Trump for President,' that 'any liability must be shifted to one or both of them'.[411]

Trump falsely claimed – as did many elected Republican officials, Trump supporters and even Fox News host Laura Ingraham – that the violence that occurred at the Capitol building was caused by left-wing agitators.[412] But participants in the Capitol siege seem to disagree. A number of people arrested for taking part in the siege have also proffered the 'Trump made me do it' defence.[413]

The way that Trump 'made them do it' was to have them believe in a 'Big Lie'.

Democratic candidate Joe Biden won the 2020 US presidential election by seven million popular votes and received 306 Electoral College votes to Trump's 232. Yet despite all evidence to the contrary, Trump continued to claim, 'I have no doubt that we won, and we won big.' His supporters believed him, too. They were primed to do so because Trump lay the groundwork for his Big Lie theory even before the election. Understanding that he would likely lose, he pre-emptively alleged fraud during the campaign and launched an online #StopTheSteal movement.[414]

To believe that the election was stolen, one had to believe that millions of votes had been altered by Democrats colluding with election officials across all 50 states, that there was a technological conspiracy to rig the election against Trump through purposely faulty electronic voting machines, and that mail-in ballots were being both under-counted and over-counted. Yet according to repeated polls, a third or more of Americans continue to believe the election was 'stolen'.[415]

The Big Lie around the election was the culmination of the myriad small and medium lies, half-truths and distortions Trump made in his public life. These included the Obama 'birther' conspiracy, in which he falsely asserted that former president Barack Obama was not born in the United States and was therefore ineligible to be elected; that Trump's inauguration crowds were the biggest; and even lies about the weather.

The Washington Post fact checker team catalogued 30,573 lies over the four years of Trump's presidency, averaging about 21 a day.[416] Trump did not stretch the truth or equivocate, as many politicians are known to do. Trump lied about things he did not have to lie about. His lies were not a character flaw or a penchant for exaggeration or even mischaracterisation. Trump's 'alternative facts' were part of his strategy to project power, troll his detractors and, most importantly, undermine democratic institutions and the checks and balances constraining him. As historian Timothy Snyder writes, 'post truth is pre fascism'.[417] Trump's lies accumulated into a lie big enough to breach the walls of American democracy.

> In the big lie there is always a certain force of credibility; because the broad masses of a nation are always more easily corrupted in the deeper strata of their emotional nature and thus in the primitive simplicity of their minds they more readily fall victims to the big lie than the small lie . . . It would never come into their heads to fabricate colossal untruths, and they would not believe others could have the impudence to distort the truth so infamously.

This passage is not an analysis of the recent American insurrection. Rather, it is taken from the writings of another figure who had 'the impudence to distort the truth'. It is from Adolf Hitler's screed *Mein Kampf*, in which he coined the term the 'big lie'. Hitler understood that the more outrageous the lie the more effective it is, so long as it taps into existing prejudices and sentiments. Hitler was not the only one to use this technique in their rise to power. It has been employed by populists and demagogues the world over, but it was used most recently and devastatingly by Trump.

Trump's Big Lie melded with another Trump-adjacent conspiracy theory movement – QAnon. Trump never explicitly endorsed the movement, but he understood his centrality to it and that a large part of his support base came from it. Trump certainly never denounced it. He flirted with the QAnon movement throughout his presidency, throwing breadcrumbs for them to pick up. When asked directly about QAnon's claims that he was 'secretly saving the world from this cult of paedophiles and cannibals,' Trump replied, 'If I can help save the world from problems, I am willing to do it . . . We are actually, we're saving the world.'[418]

QAnon supporters and their online accounts helped spread the Big Lie about the election and incorporated it into the broader Q mythology. Images of the Capitol siege show hundreds of people wearing Q t-shirts and other paraphernalia. Placards referencing QAnon slogans and memes were interspersed among the mob. The figure most associated with the Capitol siege may be the so-called 'QAnon Shaman' – the man who embodied the absurdity of QAnon, parading around Senate chambers bare chested and face painted, clad only in horns and furs.[419] One would think that the QAnon movement would finally dissipate after predictions around the election and the Day of the Rope fantasy – a reference to the mass murder of race traitors in *The Turner Diaries* – did not come to pass. Shockingly, the Public Religion Research Institute has found that support for QAnon has actually increased since Trump was voted out.[420]

QAnon has injected itself into US political parties and electoral politics. During the last election, 77 QAnon-affiliated candidates ran for Congress, two of them winning seats.[421] In the upcoming 2022 mid-term election, another 36 QAnon candidates are running as Republicans,[422] including Ron Watkins, the man believed to have started the QAnon conspiracy theory.[423] QAnon influencers and other conspiracy theorists have dominated Republican political events and conferences[424] and QAnon narratives on paedophilia and moral panic around children's safety have become mainstream Republican Party talking points.[425]

Even though the QAnon movement is US-centric, it has steadily gained a following all over the world. The QAnon conspiracy theory adapts to local conditions and preoccupations.[426] Australia has not been immune. Support down under for QAnon grew thanks to Trump's online influence and Australia's strict lockdown response to the pandemic, crossing over with anti-vaccination and anti-lockdown movements.[427] One analysis found that Australia was the fourth-largest producer of QAnon content worldwide.[428]

AUSTRALIA'S FAR RIGHT

Australia has its own long track record with right-wing extremism, white supremacy and radical right politics that long predates Trumpism.[429] But another page was written during the Trump era. Researchers at Macquarie University examined thousands of social media posts and accounts within the Australian right-wing extremist online echo chamber. Trump-related hashtags are prominent shorthand for signalling white nationalism.[430]

Trump's influence was also felt in Australian mainstream politics. Erstwhile Liberal–Nationals Coalition MPs such as Craig Kelly and George Christensen, who have now moved on to far-right minor parties, repeat Trump conspiracies and don

Make Australia Great Again hats in public appearances in a nod to Trump's MAGA slogan. The United Australia Party says it will 'Make Australia Great Again'. Former Liberal prime minister Scott Morrison refused to condemn Trump for the Capitol siege and former deputy prime minister Michael McCormack equated the storming of the Capitol with Black Lives Matter protests.[431]

Senator Pauline Hanson, leader of the One Nation party, in many ways was a precursor to Trump. She is known for parliamentary antics such as donning a burka in the Senate chamber and stripping it away in symbolic opposition to Muslim migration, raising a motion that sought to recognise the 'deplorable rise of anti-white racism and attacks on Western civilisation', and declaring that 'it is OK to be white'. One Nation is a fringe nativist party, but a dozen Coalition senators voted for her 'anti-white racism' motion, including members of the Cabinet at the time.[432] A former One Nation senator, Fraser Anning, used his inaugural speech to call for a 'final solution' to immigration.[433]

George Christensen, a one-time Nationals senator now with One Nation, appears on InfoWars with Alex Jones, a notorious right-wing radio host who peddles dangerous conspiracy theories. Christensen himself is now promoting conspiracy theories about the Covid-19 pandemic and has exploited resentment about pandemic restrictions to refashion his political career. Christensen has always courted controversy and by his own admission stokes it. But he says, 'I can be derided, Pauline and Trump can be derided. Yet all we're doing is listening to people, then repeating what they tell us they want.'[434]

One Nation and United Australia Party politicians have been regulars at anti-vax and anti-lockdown protests during the pandemic, mixing with right-wing extremists and trading in the same conspiracies and anti-Semitic messages. United Australia Party figures have reposted and endorsed content from known Australian neo-Nazis.[435]

Even if we acknowledge that One Nation and the United Australia Party sit on the far-right of Australian politics and are not supported by the majority of Australians, they have nevertheless influenced parliamentary and public debate. Governments have to negotiate with them on legislation and parliamentary procedures, and the outrage they attract fuels polarisation and impacts social cohesion.

Through these far-right politicians, positions once considered extreme have entered the mainstream. And through them, the extreme and the mainstream become entangled. They prove that, as academics Kristy Campion and Scott Poynting put it:

[T]here is no hard and fast social-scientific distinction between the extreme right and the far right, and the far right can live in symbiosis with the more conventional conservative right. These links, and their institutional arrangements enable the respectablization of the far right and 'extreme' ideologies while maintaining a hygienic distance from the (unauthorized) violence often motivated and indeed incited in far-right discourse.[436]

Though right-wing extremism is defined by its opposition to liberal democratic principles, right-wing extremists have also directly entered into Australian politics by fielding candidates and establishing minor parties. In the 2019 Australian election, a dozen far-right and extreme-right parties ran tickets.[437] Their foray into electoral politics and their efforts at political organising are an attempt to show that neo-Nazis are 'just like us' – middle-class, with families and regular jobs – in order to appeal to the mainstream.

Right-wing extremists have also tried to infiltrate established Australian right-wing parties. In 2018, extremists attempted to branch-stack both the NSW Nationals and the Liberal Party. Their aim was clearly laid out on social media in a now-deleted post: 'One of the ways to realise our goals in our lifetime is taking over an already existing party from the inside without anyone being the wiser.'[438] When it was exposed by ABC Background Briefing that the NSW branch of the Young Nationals had been infiltrated by alt-right members,[439] the individuals were thrown out and the Nationals vowed to investigate.[440] We should expect this strategy of political infiltration, coupled with the willingness to commit violence, to continue.

While seeking to enter into politics, right-wing extremists also violently target political establishments and politicians. Responding to the growing threat of violence against parliamentarians and candidates for office, for the first time the Australian Federal Police has set up a taskforce to protect federal politicians and candidates,[441] driven by growing threats from right-wing extremists and adjacent conspiracy-driven movements.[442]

*

The 2022 Australian federal election proved an important corrective to this trend of infiltration. Many far-right politicians lost their seats. The right-wing Coalition, under Scott Morrison, was routed. But during the campaign and on election day, the Coalition made a desperate attempt at a far-right appeal. Playing into Australians' longstanding concerns around border security, the party sent a text message to voters saying that an 'illegal' asylum seeker boat had been intercepted and to vote Liberal in order to keep Australia's borders secure. Morrison supported a transphobic Liberal candidate in the hopes of appealing to voters squeamish about rapidly changing gender norms. The electorate responded by rejecting Morrison's fearmongering around immigration and transgender people and delivered the Coalition a decisive loss.[443] It remains to be seen after the 2022 election whether the Coalition will return to its liberal-conservative roots or double down on far-right appeals.

What is clear is that right-wing extremism has corrupted democratic norms and mainstream politics. Many democratic governments have finally acknowledged this threat, devoting additional resources and reorienting their strategies to counter terrorism and violent extremism to address right-wing extremist violence. But violence and terrorism are only a small part of the threat right-wing extremism poses to democracy.

For one thing, much of the threat and menace from right-wing extremism does not manifest as terrorism, but rather as hate crimes, racism, homophobia, xenophobia, gendered violence and other threats to multicultural community safety and wellbeing.[444] For another, while we must suppress violent elements, we must also accommodate dissenting voices while protecting liberal democratic values and targeted groups.[445]

Democracies are in decline. Polarisation is fraying the social fabric of democracies around the world, and people are losing trust in democratic institutions to meaningfully address the major issues of the day. None of the structural issues ailing our democracies, including inequality, have been resolved or meaningfully addressed. As famed sociologist and political scientist Seymour Lipset wrote in *Some Social Requisites of Democracy*, unresolved inequalities can make democracy illegitimate to its citizens. Growing inequality, in all its guises, has left the promise of democracy unfulfilled and turned more people towards far-right populism and right-wing extremism.

To counter right-wing extremism, we cannot rely on counter-terrorism operations. We need to address democratic decline and renew our commitment to upholding multicultural, liberal, egalitarian societies. Countering right-wing extremism requires nothing short of a renewal of global democracy.

Acknowledgements

I have always been interested in extremist elements, the fringes of society, the ones who want to tear it all down. I sometimes wonder why. What is the appeal of the extreme? Part of it is a certain fascination with peering over the edge, the combined thrill and revulsion of what you find. But what it really comes down to is that, for me, the study of extremism is useful. If we want to clearly perceive the centre, we must look at it from its edges. To understand the world better, to see ourselves more clearly, it helps to examine and understand those who reject it.

For this examination of extremism, I am indebted to the many scholars, analysts and journalists who have critically examined right-wing extremism, far-right politics and populism, many of whom I cite in this book. I would also like to thank the

Lowy Institute and its Director, Michael Fullilove, for providing me with the freedom to write on a difficult and controversial subject, and Lowy Institute Research Director Hervé Lemahieu for his constructive suggestions and corrections. I would particularly like to thank Alex Oliver, an early champion. I am indebted to Sam Roggeveen, a superb editor, and Clare Caldwell, a copy editor extraordinaire. I would also like to thank Dr Mario Peucker and Kim Kane for their early reviews, encouragement and constructive suggestions and the many colleagues who provided a sounding board, exchanged ideas and helped shape my thinking on these complex issues. And to the anonymous reviewers who took time from their own projects and scholarship to make mine sharper. Their observations and suggestions for improving the manuscript were invaluable. I wish all writers a similarly exemplary reviewer experience. Any remaining errors, shortcomings or deficiencies are my own.

This book is intended to be a primer on right-wing extremism – introducing key concepts and issues to the interested reader. I also sought to particularly focus on its modern trajectory and unique threat to democracy. There are many elements and dynamics of right-wing extremism that I was not able to cover in this volume. However, the gaps in this book are more than filled by the rich historical, research-based and journalistic efforts of many others.

Completing a major project, like writing a book, is not possible without the reinforcement of those closest to you. For that I would like to especially thank my family: the wise counsel and support of my husband, Peter, who also picked up the slack on the home front while juggling his own professional responsibilities; my mother, Sophia, who upended her own life to support us; and especially my children, who not only tolerated my absences from them while I drafted this manuscript, but who would inquire after my progress and often put me in 'writing jail' so I could finish. Their love, encouragement and curiosity inspire me always.

Endnotes

1. 'Faith and Fury: Sheryl Stack's Story', CNN, 16 April 2012, https://edition.cnn.com/videos/us/2012/04/16/cnn-presents-faith-and-fury-1.cnn.

2. Dave Cullen, 'Seven Deadly Traits: Decoding the Confession of the Austin Plane Bomber', *Slate*, 19 February 2010, https://slate.com/news-and-politics/2010/02/decoding-the-confession-of-joseph-stack.html.

3. 'Death and Taxes: Joe Stack's Attack on the IRS', CNN Special Investigation, 18 April 2010, http://edition.cnn.com/TRANSCRIPTS/1004/18/siu.01.html.

4. Untitled suicide note of Joseph Stack, 18 February 2010 in Richard Adams, 'Joseph Stack's Suicide Note', *The Guardian*, 19 February 2010, https://www.theguardian.com/world/richard-adams-blog/2010/feb/18/austin-irs-joseph-stack.

5. 'Death and Taxes: Joe Stack's Attack on the IRS'.

6. 'Faith and Fury: Sheryl Stack's Story'.

7. Michael Brick, 'Man Crashes Plane into Texas IRS Office', *The New York Times*, 18 February 2010, https://www.nytimes.com/2010/02/19/us/19crash.html.

8. Richard Whittaker, 'The T Word: Politicians and Media Dance around What to Call the Plane Crash', *The Austin Chronicle*, 19 February 2010, https://www.austinchronicle.com/daily/news/2010-02-19/the-t-word/.

9. Untitled suicide note of Joseph Stack, 18 February 2010.

10. Janet Napolitano, 'The 16th Anniversary of the Oklahoma City Bombing', 19 April 2011, https://www.dhs.gov/blog/2011/04/19/16th-anniversary-oklahoma-city-bombing.

11. Spencer S. Hsu, 'Napolitano Rules out Terrorism in IRS Plane Crash', *The Washington Post*, 9 March 2010, http://voices.washingtonpost.com/44/2010/03/napolitano-rules-out-terrorism.html?wprss=44.

12. Mark Pitcavage, 'Cerberus Unleashed: The Three Faces of the Lone Wolf Terrorist', *American Behavioral Scientist*, 59, No.13 (2015):1655–1680.

13. Mark Potok, 'Austin Killer Becoming a Hero to the Radical Right', *Hate Watch Blog*, Southern Poverty Law Center, 19 February 2010, https://www.splcenter.org/hatewatch/2010/02/19/austin-killer-becoming-hero-radical-right.

14. 'Congressman Wants Light Airplane Security Review', *AV Web*, 21 February 2010, https://www.avweb.com/news/congressman-wants-light-airplane-security-review/.

15. US Department of Homeland Security, *Rightwing Extremism: Current Economic and Political Climate Fueling Resurgence in Radicalization and Recruitment*, Office of Intelligence and Analysis Assessment, DHS/ I&A Production Branch, IA-0257-09, (Washington. DC: DHS Office of Intelligence and Analysis, 7 April 2009), https://irp.fas.org/eprint/rightwing.pdf.

16. Brett Murphy, Will Carless, Marisa Kwiatkowski and Tricia Nadolny, 'A 2009 Warning about Right-Wing Extremism was Engulfed in Politics. There are Signs it's Happening Again', *USA Today,* 25 January 2021, https://www.usatoday.com/story/ news/investigations/2021/01/25/twelve-years- before-capitol-riot-warning-right-wing-extremism- buried/6658284002/.

17. Teddy Davis and Ferdous Al-Faruque, 'Napolitano Facing Republican Calls for Her Ouster', ABC News, 24 April 2009, https://abcnews.go.com/Politics/ story?id=7412992&page=1.

18. 'Homeland Security Chief Apologies to Veterans Groups', CNN, 16 April 2009, http://edition.cnn. com/2009/POLITICS/04/16/napolitano.apology/.

19. Daryl Johnson, 'Inside the DHS: Former Top Analyst Says Agency Bowed to Political Pressure', Interview by Heidi Beirich, Intelligence Report, Southern Poverty Law Center, 17 June 2011, https://www.splcenter.org/ fighting-hate/intelligence-report/2011/inside-dhs-former- top-analyst-says-agency-bowed-political-pressure.

20. Daryl Johnson, 'I Warned of Right-Wing Violence in 2009. Republicans Objected. I was Right',

The Washington Post, 21 August 2017, https://www.
washingtonpost.com/news/posteverything/wp/2017/
08/21/i-warned-of-right-wing-violence-in-2009-it-
caused-an-uproar-i-was-right/.

21. Mark Potok et al, *The Second Wave: Return of the
Militias,* Southern Poverty Law Center, (Alabama:
Southern Poverty Law Center, August 2009), https://
www.splcenter.org/sites/default/files/d6_legacy_files/
downloads/The_Second_Wave.pdf.

22. Interview with Senator Scott Brown, Fox News,
19 February 2010, https://www.youtube.com/
watch?v=EEDXW87ptFU.

23. Julie Zauzmer Weil, 'Following the Pittsburgh Attack,
Rep. Steve King's Iowa Supporters Brush Aside Concern
about His White Nationalist Views', *The Washington
Post,* 28 October 2018, https://www.washingtonpost.
com/politics/in-the-wake-of-the-pittsburgh-attack-rep-
steve-kings-iowa-supporters-brush-aside-concern-about-
his-white-nationalist-views/2018/10/28/a16b7044-dabf-
11e8-b732-3c72cbf131f2_story.html.

24. Lee Fang, 'Rep. King Justifies Suicide Attack on
IRS: Sympathizes with Hatred of IRS, Hopes for its
Destruction', *Think Progress,* 22 February 2010, https://
archive.thinkprogress.org/rep-king-justifies-suicide-
attack-on-irs-sympathizes-with-hatred-of-irs-hopes-for-
its-destruction-63a6cdbd1b7e/.

25. 'Congressman: 'Implode' More IRS Offices', *Daily
Beast,* 25 April 2017, https://www.thedailybeast.com/
cheats/2010/02/23/congressman-lsquoimplodersquo-
more-irs-offices?social=Linkedin&via=desktop.

26. Robert O'Harrow, Andrew Ba Tran and Derek Hawkins, 'The Rise of Domestic Extremism in America', *The Washington Post,* 12 April 2021, https://www.washingtonpost.com/investigations/interactive/2021/domestic-terrorism-data/.

27. US Department of Homeland Security, *Homeland Security Threat Assessment*, (Washington, DC: Department of Homeland Security, October 2020), https://www.dhs.gov/sites/default/files/publications/2020_10_06_homeland-threat-assessment.pdf.

28. Federal Bureau of Investigation and Department of Homeland Security, *Strategic Intelligence Assessment and Data on Domestic Terrorism*, submitted to the Permanent Select Committee on Intelligence, the Committee on Homeland Security, and the Committee of the Judiciary of the US House of Representatives and the Select Committee on Intelligence, the Committee on Homeland Security and Government Affairs, and the Committee of the Judiciary of the United States Senate, (Washington, DC: Federal Bureau of Investigation and Department of Homeland Security, May 2021), https://www.fbi.gov/file-repository/fbi-dhs-domestic-terrorism-strategic-report.pdf/view.

29. Glenn Kessler, 'The 'Very Fine People' at Charlottesville: Who Were They?', *The Washington Post,* 8 May 2020, https://www.washingtonpost.com/politics/2020/05/08/very-fine-people-charlottesville-who-were-they-2/.

30. *Final Report: Independent Review of the 2017 Protest Events in Charlottesville, Virginia*, (Hunton & Williams, LLP, 24 November 2017), https://www.policinginstitute.org/wp-content/uploads/2017/12/Charlottesville-Critical-Incident-Review-2017.pdf

31. Kessler, 'The 'Very Fine People' at Charlottesville: Who Were They?'.

32. '2017 Audit of Anti-Semitic Incidents', ADL Center on Extremism, 25 February 2018, https://www.adl.org/resources/report/2017-audit-anti-semitic-incidents.

33. Jeff Desjardins, 'Mapped: The World's Oldest Democracies', World Economic Forum, 8 August 2019, https://www.weforum.org/agenda/2019/08/countries-are-the-worlds-oldest-democracies.

34. *Member States Concerned by the Growing and Increasingly Transnational Threat of Extremism Right-Wing Terrorism*, CTED Trends Alert, (United Nations Security Council Counter-Terrorism Committee Executive Directorate, April 2020), https://www.statewatch.org/media/documents/news/2020/apr/un-cted-trend-alert-right-wing-extremism-4-20.pdf.

35. Ibid.

36. Statement by Mike Burgess, Director-General ASIO, 'PJCIS Inquiry into Extremist Movements and Radicalisation in Australia', Australian Security Intelligence Organisation, 29 April 2021, https://www.asio.gov.au/publications/speeches-and-statements/pjcis-inquiry-extremist-movements-and-radicalisation-australia.html.

37. Alex Mann and Kevin Nguyen, 'The Base Tapes', ABC Background Briefing, 26 March 2021, https://www.abc.net.au/news/2021-03-26/the-base-tapes-secret-recordings-australian-recruitment/13255994.

38. Jacob Aasland Ravndal, Madeleine Thorstensen, Anders Ravik Jupskås and Graham Macklin, *RTV Trend Report 2021: Right-Wing Terrorism and Violence in Western Europe, 1990–2020*, C-Rex Research Report, No.1/2021, (University of Oslo, 2021), https://www.sv.uio.no/c-rex/english/publications/c-rex-reports/2021/rtv-trend-report/c-rex-rtv-trend-report-2021.pdf.

39. Laurenz Gehrke, 'Germany Records Highest Level of Right-Wing Extremist Crime in 20 Years', *Politico*, 4 May 2021, https://www.politico.eu/article/germany-records-highest-level-of-right-wing-extremist-crimes-in-20-years/.

40. Ezel Sahinkaya, 'Germany Dissolves Elite Army Unit over Far-Right Activity', *Voice of America News*, 1 August 2020, https://www.voanews.com/a/extremism-watch_germany-dissolves-elite-army-unit-over-far-right-activity/6193792.html.

41. Government of India, Ministry of Home Affairs, Minister of Home Affairs, Response to Lok Sabha Unstarred Question No.4277, 'Riots and Lynching Incidents', 29 March 2022, http://164.100.24.220/loksabhaquestions/annex/178/AU4277.pdf.

42. Praveen Swami, 'India's Turned a Blind Right Eye to Hindutva Violence, but It Can be a Threat to the State Itself', *The Print*, 17 April 2022, https://theprint.in/opinion/security-code/indias-turned-a-blind-right-eye-to-hindutva-violence-but-it-can-be-a-threat-to-state-itself/918092/.

43. 'Narendra Modi's Sectarianism is Eroding India's Secular Democracy', *The Economist*, 24 January 2020,

https://www.economist.com/briefing/2020/01/23/narendra-modis-sectarianism-is-eroding-indias-secular-democracy.

44. Julian E. Barnes and Hailey Fuchs, 'White House Orders Assessment on Violent Extremism in US', *The New York Times,* 22 January 2021, https://www.nytimes.com/2021/01/22/us/politics/capitol-riot-domestic-extremism.html.

45. White House National Security Council, *National Strategy for Countering Domestic Terrorism,* (Washington, DC, National Security Council, June 2021), https://www.whitehouse.gov/wp-content/uploads/2021/06/National-Strategy-for-Countering-Domestic-Terrorism.pdf.

46. Sam Jackson, *A Schema of Right-Wing Extremism in the United States*, ICCT Policy Brief, October 2019, (The Hague: International Centre for Counter-Terrorism, October 2019), https://icct.nl/app/uploads/2019/11/ASchemaofRWEXSamJackson-1.pdf.

47. Elisabeth Carter, 'Right-Wing Extremism/Radicalism: Reconstructing the Concept', *Journal of Political Ideologies,* 23, No.2, 157–182 (2018).

48. *Member States Concerned by the Growing and Increasingly Transnational Threat of Extreme Right-Wing Terrorism*, CTED Trends Alert.

49. Norberto Bobbio, *Left and Right: The Significance of a Political Distinction,* Translated by Allan Cameron, (Chicago: University of Chicago Press, 1993).

50. Cas Mudde, *The Far Right Today*, (Oxford: Polity, 2019).

51. Cas Mudde, 'The Far Right and the European Elections', *Current History*, 113, No.761, 98–103, (2014).

52. Jackson, *A Schema of Right-Wing Extremism in the United States*.

53. Brenton Tarrant, 'The Great Replacement', March, 2019.

54. Jackson, *A Schema of Right-Wing Extremism in the United States*.

55. Carter, 'Right-Wing Extremism/Radicalism: Reconstructing the Concept'.

56. J. M. Berger, *Extremism*, (Cambridge: MIT Press, 2018).

57. Yasmine Ahmed and Orla Lynch, 'Terrorism Studies and the Far Right – The State of Play', *Studies in Conflict and Terrorism*, 11 August 2021, https://doi.org/10.1080/1057610X.2021.1956063.

58. Berger, *Extremism*.

59. Seymour Martin Lipset and Earl Raab, *The Politics of Unreason: Right-Wing Extremism in America, 1790–1970*, (New York: Harper and Row, 1970); and Richard Hofstadter, 'Paranoid Style in American Politics', *Harper's Magazine*, November 1964, https://harpers.org/archive/1964/11/the-paranoid-style-in-american-politics/.

60. Sander van der Linden, Costas Panagopoulos, Flávio Azevedo and John T. Jost, 'The Paranoid Style in American Politics Revisited: An Ideological Asymmetry in Conspiratorial Thinking', *Political Psychology*, 42, No.1, 23–51, (2020), https://doi.org/10.1111/pops.12681.

61. Annelies Pauwels, *Contemporary Manifestations of Violent Right-Wing Extremism in the EU: An Overview of P/CVE Practices*, Radicalisation Awareness Network Report, (Luxembourg: Publications Office of the European Union, 2021), https://ec.europa.eu/home-affairs/system/files/2021-04/ran_adhoc_cont_manif_vrwe_eu_overv_pcve_pract_2021_en.pdf.

62. Federal Bureau of Investigation and Department of Homeland Security, *Strategic Intelligence Assessment and Data on Domestic Terrorism*.

63. Maani Truu, 'Threats from Far-Right Extremists have Skyrocketed in Australia, with ASIO Comparing Tactics to IS', SBS News, 22 September 2020, https://www.sbs.com.au/news/threats-from-far-right-extremists-have-skyrocketed-in-australia-with-asio-comparing-tactics-to-is/129ae926-15f0-4984-a935-3fc4678e2fa8.

64. Professor Michele Grossman, interview with author, 27 April 2021.

65. Shiraz Maher, *Salafi-Jihadism: The History of an Idea*, (New York: Oxford University Press, 2016).

66. It is important to note that reception among the Muslim community to this change was mixed. While some community figures welcomed the change, they also noted the need to adjust departmental priorities to counter the right-wing extremist threat and explicitly label it as such. Others identified this change as first and foremost motivated by political pressure to appease far-right political figures. See: Lydia Khalil, 'Far Right Angles', *The Saturday Paper*, No. 347, 1–7 May 2019.

67. Khalil, 'Far Right Angles'.

68. Michael McGowan, 'Adelaide Man Arrested for Allegedly Possessing Improvised Explosive Device in Far-Right Raids', *The Guardian*, 8 April 2021, https://www.theguardian.com/australia-news/2021/apr/08/adelaide-man-arrested-for-allegedly-possessing-improvised-explosive-device-in-far-right-raids.

69. Nick McKenzie and Joel Tozer, 'Neo-Nazis Go Bush: Grampians Gathering Highlights Rise of Australia's Far Right', *The Age*, 27 January 2021, https://www.theage.com.au/politics/federal/neo-nazis-go-bush-grampians-gathering-highlights-rise-of-australia-s-far-right-20210127-p56xbf.html.

70. Mike Burgess, Parliament of Australia, Estimates – Home Affairs Portfolio, Australian Security Intelligence Organisation, Legal and Constitutional Affairs Legislation Committee, 2 March 2020, https://www.aph.gov.au/Parliamentary_Business/Hansard/Hansard_Display?bid=committees/estimate/9cba4477-60ef-40db-a537-241108688a6c/&sid=0006.

71. Sebastian Rotella, 'Global Right-Wing Extremism Networks are Growing. The US is Just Now Catching Up', *ProPublica*, 22 January 2021, https://www.propublica.org/article/global-right-wing-extremism-networks-are-growing-the-u-s-is-just-now-catching-up.

72. Australian Security Intelligence Organisation, *ASIO Annual Report 2019–20*, (Australian Security Intelligence Organisation: Commonwealth of Australia, 2020), https://www.asio.gov.au/sites/default/files/ASIO%20Annual%20Report%202019-20.pdf.

73. Tarrant, 'The Great Replacement'.

74. 'Sens. Cruz, Cassidy: Antifa is a Domestic Terrorist Organization', Press Release, Office of Senator Ted Cruz, 18 July 2019, https://www.cruz.senate.gov/newsroom/press-releases/sens-cruz-cassidy-antifa-is-a-domestic-terrorist-organization.

75. Leslie Gornstein, 'What is Antifa? Is it a Group or an Idea, and What Do Supporters Want?', CBS News, 29 March 2021, https://www.cbsnews.com/news/what-is-antifa/.

76. Mario Peucker and Jacob Davey, 'Does Australia's Radical Left Pose a Security Threat? What Does the Empirical Evidence Tell Us?', ABC Religion and Ethics, 15 December 2020, https://www.abc.net.au/religion/does-the-radical-left-pose-a-security-threat-to-australia/12987240.

77. Stanislav Vysotsky, *American Antifa: The Tactics, Culture, and Practice of Militant Antifascism,* (Routledge: 2020).

78. Khalil, 'Far Right Angles'.

79. Cas Mudde, *Populist Radical Right Parties in Europe,* (Cambridge: Cambridge University Press, 2007).

80. Cynthia Miller-Idriss, *Hate in the Homeland: The New Global Far Right,* (Princeton: Princeton University Press, 2020).

81. Ibid.

82. Glen Weldon, 'Superheroes and the F-Word: Grappling with the Ugly Truth under the Capes', *Pop Culture*

Happy Hour, National Public Radio, 16 November 2016, https://www.npr.org/2016/11/16/502161587/superheroes-and-the-f-word-grappling-with-the-ugly-truth-under-the-capes.

83. Hannah Allam and Razzan Nakhlawi, 'Black, Brown and Extremist: Across the Far-Right Spectrum, People of Color Play a More Visible Role', *The Washington Post*, 16 May 2021, https://www.washingtonpost.com/national-security/minorities-far-right-visible-role/2021/05/16/e7ba8338-a915-11eb-8c1a-56f0cb4ff3b5_story.html.

84. Dani Rodrik, 'Why Does Globalisation Fuel Populism? Economics, Culture, and the Rise of Right-Wing Populism', *Annual Review of Economics*, 13, 133–170, (2021), https://doi.org/10.1146/annurev-economics-070220-032416.

85. Matthew Sharpe, 'Understanding the Appeal of the Extreme Right is Key to Preventing Its Resurgence', ABC Religion and Ethics, 21 October 2021, https://www.abc.net.au/religion/matthew-sharpe-understanding-appeal-of-extreme-right/13596814.

86. Syed Mansoob Murshed, 'Global Inequality in the New Dark Age of Extremism', Vision of Humanity, https://www.visionofhumanity.org/inequality-age-extremism-economists-peace/.

87. Facundo Alvaredo, Lucas Chancel, Thomas Piketty, Emmanuel Saez and Gabriel Zucman, *World Inequality Report*, World Inequality Lab, (Paris: World Inequality Lab, 2018), https://wir2018.wid.world/files/download/wir2018-full-report-english.pdf.

88. Thomas Piketty, *Capital and Ideology,* (Cambridge: Harvard University Press, 2020).

89. Alan de Bromhead, Barry Eichengreen and Kevin H. O'Rourke, 'Right-Wing Political Extremism in the Great Depression', National Bureau of Economic Research, Working Paper 17871, February 2012, https://www.nber.org/papers/w17871.

90. The 2008 Global Financial Crisis not only led to support for populist far-right political parties and movements but also led to street violence and violent anti-government protests. Because financial crises usually result from elite policy failures and moral hazards, and typically involve bailouts for the unpopular financial sector, they trigger greater political dissatisfaction and more fractured parliaments. These fractured parliaments are less likely able to pass the necessary legislation and policy platforms needed to address the problems wrought from the financial crisis, creating a vicious cycle of political and institutional ineffectiveness. See Atif Mian, Amir Sufi and Francesco Trebbi, 'Resolving Debt Overhang: Political Constraints in the Aftermath of Financial Crises', *American Economic Journal,* 6, No.2, (April, 2014): 1–28.

91. Thomas Piketty, 'Brahmin Left vs Merchant Right: Rising Inequality & the Changing Structure of Political Conflict', WID.World Working Paper, Series No. 2018/7, World Inequality Lab, March, 2018, http://129.199.194.17/files/Piketty2018.pdf.

92. Liz Fekete, 'Flying the Flag for Neoliberalism', *Race and Class,* 58, No.3 (January 2017): 3–22, https://doi.org/10.1177/0306396816670088.

93. Michael Barkun, *A Culture of Conspiracy: Apocalyptic Visions in Contemporary America*, (Berkeley: University of California Press, 2013).

94. 'Why is 'New World Order' Ideology Spreading?', CBS News, 6 November 2013, https://www.cbsnews.com/video/why-is-new-world-order-ideology-spreading/#x.

95. Rodrik, 'Why Does Globalization Fuel Populism?'.

96. Alan B. Krueger and Jitka Malečková. 'Education, Poverty and Terrorism: Is There a Causal Connection?', *The Journal of Economic Perspectives*, 17, No.4 (2003): 119–44.

97. Sophie Kaldor, *Far-Right Violent Extremism as a Failure of Status: A New Approach to Extremist Manifestos through the Lens of Ressentiment*, ICCT Research Paper, May 2021, (The Hague: International Centre for Counter-Terrorism, May 2021), https://icct.nl/app/uploads/2021/05/Far-Right-Violent-Extremism-as-a-Failure-of-Status.pdf.

98. Martha Crenshaw, *Explaining Terrorism: Causes, Processes and Consequences,* (London and New York: Routledge, 2011).

99. Joey Watson, 'Everyone Wants to be Fuhrer, Part 2', ABC Radio National, *Earshot*, 14 March 2022, https://www.abc.net.au/radionational/programs/earshot/everyone-wants-to-be-fuhrer-ep-2/13785880.

100. Jan-Willem van Prooijen and Mark van Vugt. 'Conspiracy Theories: Evolved Functions and

Psychological Mechanisms', *Perspectives on Psychological Science*, 13, No.6 (November 2018): 770–88, https://doi.org/10.1177/1745691618774270.

101. '1st WHO Infodemiology Conference', World Health Organization, 30 June–16 July 2020, https://www. who.int/news-room/events/detail/2020/06/30/default-calendar/1st-who-infodemiology-conference.

102. 'Infodemic', World Health Organization, https://www. who.int/health-topics/infodemic.

103. Lydia Khalil, 'The Impact of Natural Disasters on Violent Extremism', ASPI Counterterrorism Yearbook 2021, ed. Leanne Close and Daria Impiombato, Australian Strategic Policy Institute, March 2021, https://www.aspi. org.au/report/counterterrorism-yearbook-2021.

104. Lydia Khalil, Submission to the Parliamentary Joint Committee on Intelligence and Security, Inquiry into Extremist Movements and Radicalism in Australia, (Sydney: Lowy Institute, February 2021), https:// www.lowyinstitute.org/sites/default/files/KHALIL%20 PJCIS%20Parliamentary%20Submission%20 FINAL%20PDF.pdf.

105. Jan-Willem van Prooijen and Karen Douglas, 'Belief in Conspiracy Theories: Basic Principles of an Emerging Research Domain', *European Journal of Social Psychology,* 48, No.7, (August, 2018), 897–908, https://doi.org/10.1002/ejsp.2530.

106. Marina Abalakina-Paap, Walter G. Stephan, Traci Craig and W. Larry Gregory, 'Beliefs in Conspiracies', *Political Psychology,* 20, No.3, (December, 2002) 637–647, https://doi.org/10.1111/0162-895X.00160.

107. Benjamin Lee, 'Radicalisation and Conspiracy Theories', in *Routledge Handbook of Conspiracy Theories*, ed. Michael Butter and Peter Knight, (Abingdon: Routledge, 2020), 344–356.

108. Bettina Rottweiler and Paul Gill, 'Conspiracy Beliefs and Violent Extremist Intentions: The Contingent Effects of SelfEfficacy, SelfControl and LawRelated Morality', *Terrorism and Political Violence*, (2020), https://doi.org/10.1080/09546553. 2020.1803288.

109. Lipset and Raab, *The Politics of Unreason*.

110. Anna Merlan, 'The Conspiracy Singularity Has Arrived', *Vice News*, 18 July 2020, https://www.vice. com/en/article/v7gz53/the-conspiracy-singularity-has-arrived.

111. Marc-André Argentino, 'In the Name of the Father, Son, and Q: Why It's Important to See QAnon as a 'Hyper-Real' Religion', *Religion Dispatches*, 28 May 2020, https://religiondispatches.org/in-the-name-of-the-father-son-and-q-why-its-important-to-see-qanon-as-a-hyper-real-religion/.

112. Nick Backovic, Jordan Wildon and Joe Ondrak, 'Logically Identifies GhostEzra, Florida Man behind World's 'Largest Antisemitic Internet Forum", *Logically*, 20 August 2021, https://www.logically. ai/articles/exclusive-ghostezra-florida-man-largest-antisemitic-forum.

113. Patrick Crusius, 'The Inconvenient Truth', August 2019.

114. Bernhard Forchtner, 'The Far Right has Moved from Climate Denial to Obstructing Climate Action', Open Democracy, 1 November 2021, https://www.opendemocracy.net/en/author/berhard-forchtner/.

115. Alexander Reid Ross and Emmi Bevensee, 'Confronting the Rise of Eco-Fascism Means Grappling with Complex Systems', CARR Research Insight, Centre for Analysis of Radical Right, July 2020, https://www.radicalrightanalysis.com/wp-content/uploads/2020/07/Ross_Bevensee_2020.3.pdf.

116. Peter Staudenmaier, 'Understanding Right-Wing Ecology: Historical and Contemporary Reflections', *Ideology Theory Practice,* 26 July 2021, https://www.ideology-theory-practice.org/blog/understanding-right-wing-ecology-historical-and-contemporary-reflections#_ftn21.

117. Posts from 'Australian Ecofascist Memes', Facebook.

118. Note the reference to left-wing ideological terms such as 'proletariat' and 'class warfare'. This is a deliberate tactic used by right-wing extremists to confuse people, such as the former Senator, into making an association of these movements with left-wing extremism. See Mark Greenblatt and Lauren Knapp, 'Extremist Heimbach to Relaunch Hate Group, Says He Supports Violence', Interview with Matthew Heimbach, *Newsy,* 20 July 2021, https://www.newsy.com/stories/extremist-heimbach-to-relaunch-hate-group-supports-violence-3/.

119. Ronald Reagan, Presidential News Conference, 12 August 1986, https://www.reaganfoundation.org/ronald-reagan/reagan-quotes-speeches/news-conference-1/.

120. Richard Wike, Laura Silver and Alexandra Castillo, 'Many across the Globe are Dissatisfied with How Democracy is Working', Pew Research Center, 29 April 2019, https://www.pewresearch.org/global/2019/04/29/many-across-the-globe-are-dissatisfied-with-how-democracy-is-working/.

121. 'Democracies in Decline', Freedom House, https://freedomhouse.org/issues/democracies-decline, accessed 12 March 2022.

122. Sarah Repucci and Amy Slipowitz, 'Democracy under Siege', Freedom in the World 2021, Freedom House, March 2021, https://freedomhouse.org/sites/default/files/2021-03/FIW2021_Abridged_03112021_FINAL.pdf.

123. Ibid.

124. *Annual Outcomes Report 2020: Defending Democracy*, International Institute for Democracy and Electoral Assistance, 27 April 2021, https://www.idea.int/reference_docs/annual-outcome-report-2020-defending-democracy.

125. Ibid.

126. *Democracy Index 2020: In Sickness and in Health?*, Economist Intelligence Unit, (2020), https://www.eiu.com/n/campaigns/democracy-index-2020/.

127. Ibid.

128. Jenny Chesters, 'Egalitarian Australia? Associations between Family Wealth and Outcomes in Young

Adulthood', *Journal of Sociology,* 55, No.1 (March 2019): 72–89, https://doi.org/10.1177/144078 3318777293.

129. Mark Evans, Will Jennings and Gerry Stoker, 'How Does Australia Compare: What Makes a Leading Democracy?', *Democracy 2025,* Report No.6, https://www.democracy2025.gov.au/documents/ Democracy2025-report6.pdf.

130. 'Le Pen Claims Increase in Vote Share in 2022 Election as Victory in Itself', ABC News, 25 April 2022, https:// www.abc.net.au/news/2022-04-25/la-pen-increseases-vote-share-in-2022-election/13853306.

131. 'Jeff Schoep, Extremist Info', Southern Poverty Law Center, https://www.splcenter.org/fighting-hate/ extremist-files/individual/jeff-schoep.

132. John Eligon, 'He Says His Nazi Days are over. Do You Believe Him?', *The New York Times,* 4 April 2020, https://www.nytimes.com/2020/04/04/us/jeff-schoep-white-nationalist-reformer.html.

133. Deeyah Khan, 'White Right: Meeting the Enemy', Exposure, Season 7, Episode 2, air date 11 December 2017, https://www.imdb.com/title/tt7750864/.

134. Eligon, 'He Says His Nazi Days Are Over'.

135. Jeff Schoep, interview with author, 3 December 2021.

136. Ibid.

137. Ibid.

138. Jung-Kyoo Choi and Samuel Bowles, 'The Coevolution of Parochial Altruism and War', *Science,* 318, No.5850, (October 2017) 636–640, https://www.science.org/doi/abs/10.1126/science.1144237.

139. Jeff Schoep, 'In and Out of White Supremacist Movements: Lessons from the United States', Centre for Resilient and Inclusive Societies, Webinar, 27 October 2021.

140. Leor Zmigrod, Ian W. Eisenberg, Patrick G. Bissett, Trevor W. Robbins and Russell A. Poldrack, 'The Cognitive and Perceptual Correlates of Ideological Attitudes: A Data-Driven Approach', *Philosophical Transactions of the Royal Society*, 22 February 2021, https://royalsocietypublishing.org/doi/10.1098/rstb.2020.0424.

141. David Webber and Arie W. Kruglanski, 'Psychological Factors in Radicalization: A '3N' Approach', in *The Handbook of the Criminology of Terrorism*, eds. Gary LaFree and Joshua Freilich, (West Sussex: Wiley Blackwell, 2017), 33–46.

142. Jeff Schoep, interview with author, 3 December 2021.

143. Andrew Lapin, 'The Ex-Nazi Next Door', *The Detroit Jewish News,* 21 May 2020, https://thejewishnews.com/2020/05/21/the-ex-nazi-next-door/.

144. Paul M. Sniderman, Louk Hagendoorn and Markus Prior, 'Predisposing Factors and Situational Triggers: Exclusionary Reactions to Immigrant Minorities,' *American Political Science Review*, 98,

No.1 (2004): 35–49, https://www.cambridge.org/core/journals/american-political-science-review/article/abs/predisposing-factors-and-situational-triggers-exclusionary-reactions-to-immigrant-minorities/8E06A1959ACC771754651B897E8E24A8.

145. William H. Frey, 'The Nation is Diversifying Even Faster than Predicted, According to New Census Data', Brookings Institution, 1 July 2020, https://www.brookings.edu/research/new-census-data-shows-the-nation-is-diversifying-even-faster-than-predicted/.

146. Andrew H. Kydd, 'Decline, Radicalization and the Attack on the US Capitol', *Violence: An International Journal*, 2, No.1 (April 2021): 3–23, https://journals.sagepub.com/doi/10.1177/26330024211010043.

147. Jan-Willem van Prooijen, André Krouwel and Julia Emmer, 'Ideological Responses to the EU Refugee Crisis: The Left, the Right, and the Extremes', *Social Psychological and Personality Science,* 9, No.2, (2017), 143–150, https://journals.sagepub.com/doi/pdf/10.1177/1948550617731501.

148. Australian Institute of Health and Welfare, 'Profile of Australia's Population', Snapshot, 16 September 2021, https://www.aihw.gov.au/reports/australias-welfare/profile-of-australias-population.

149. Australian Bureau of Statistics, 'Statistics on Australia's International Migration, Internal Migration (Interstate and Intrastate) and the Population by Country of Birth, 2019–2020 Financial Year', 23 June 2021, https://www.abs.gov.au/statistics/people/population/migration-australia/latest-release#net-overseas-migration.

150. Andrew Markus, *Mapping Social Cohesion: The Scanlon Foundation Surveys – 2020*, (Caulfield East: Monash University, 2021), https://scanloninstitute.org.au/report2020.

151. Ibid.

152. Shannon Molloy, 'The New Extremist Threat in Australia: Right-Wing Groups Who have ASIO's Attention', News.com.au, 4 January 2019, https://www.news.com.au/national/the-new-extremist-threat-in-australia-rightwing-groups-who-have-asios-attention/news-story/44ae06be0aaa765c862fd6d20426fe9a.

153. Blair Cottrell, appearance on *The Adam Giles Show*, Sky News, 5 August 2018.

154. Lara Bullens, 'How France's 'Great Replacement' Theory Conquered the Global Far Right', France 24, 8 November 2021, https://www.france24.com/en/europe/20211108-how-the-french-great-replacement-theory-conquered-the-far-right.

155. Jacob Davey and Julia Ebner, *'The Great Replacement': The Violent Consequences of Mainstreamed Extremism*, Institute for Strategic Dialogue, (London: Institute for Strategic Dialogue, 2019), https://www.isdglobal.org/wp-content/uploads/2019/07/The-Great-Replacement-The-Violent-Consequences-of-Mainstreamed-Extremism-by-ISD.pdf.

156. David Holthouse, 'Full of Ship: Behind Generation Identity's High Seas Publicity Stunt', *Hatewatch Blog*,

Southern Poverty Law Center, 13 November 2017, https://www.splcenter.org/hatewatch/2017/11/13/full-ship-behind-generation-identitys-high-seas-publicity-stunt.

157. Andy Gregory, 'Members of Far-Right Group Generation Identity Jailed after Anti-Migrant Operation in French Alps', *The Independent,* 30 August 2019, https://www.independent.co.uk/news/world/europe/far-right-generation-identity-members-jailed-alps-france-asylum-seekers-a9084976.html.

158. Imogen Richards, 'A Philosophical and Historical Analysis of 'Generation Identity': Fascism, Online Media, and the European New Right', *Terrorism and Political Violence*, 34, No.1, 30 September 2019, 28–47, https://www.tandfonline.com/doi/full/10.1080/09546553.2019.1662403.

159. 'Generation Hate', Al Jazeera Investigation, 10 December 2018, https://www.aljazeera.com/news/2018/12/10/what-is-generation-identity.

160. Davey and Ebner, *'The Great Replacement'*.

161. 'Generation Hate', Al Jazeera Investigation.

162. 'The Great Replacement: An Explainer', Anti-Defamation League, 19 April 2021, https://www.adl.org/resources/backgrounders/the-great-replacement-an-explainer.

163. Royal Commission of Inquiry into the Terrorist Attack on Christchurch Mosques on 15 March

2019, The Report, Part 4: The Terrorist, Chapter 4: General Life in New Zealand, 21 December 2020, https://christchurchattack.royalcommission.nz/ the-report/firearms-licensing/general-life-in-new- zealand/,

164. 'Generation Identity: France Shuts Down Far-Right Group', Al Jazeera, Investigation, 3 March 2021, https://www.aljazeera.com/news/2021/3/3/generation- identity-france-shuts-down-far-right-group.

165. French Ministry of Interior, Notice Letter to M. Clément Gandelin, President Génération Identitaire, 11 February 2021, https://www.documentcloud.org/ documents/20489793-generation-identify-shutdown- process-to-begin.

166. Davey and Ebner, *'The Great Replacement'*.

167. Harris Interactive Poll, *'L'opinion concernat la possibilite d'un 'gran remplacement'*, 21 October 2021, https://twitter.com/harrisint_fr/status/1450816889790 337025?s=20.

168. Didier Fassin, 'The Rise of Éric Zemmour Shows How Far France has Shifted to the Right', *The Guardian*, 1 December 2021, https://www.theguardian.com/ commentisfree/2021/dec/01/eric-zemmour-france-right- presidential-candidate.

169. Bullens, 'How France's 'Great Replacement' Theory Conquered the Global Far Right'.

170. Holthouse, 'Full of Ship'.

171. Daniel Lombroso, 'Why the Alt-Right's Most Famous Woman Disappeared', *The Atlantic,* 16 October 2020, https://www.theatlantic.com/politics/archive/2020/10/alt-right-star-racist-propagandist-has-no-regrets/616725/.

172. Holthouse, 'Full of Ship'.

173. Karen Yourish et al, 'Inside the Apocalyptic Worldview of Tucker Carlson Tonight', *The New York Times,* 30 April 2022, https://www.nytimes.com/interactive/2022/04/30/us/tucker-carlson-tonight.html?chapter=3.

174. Lis Power, 'Fox News 'Invasion' Rhetoric by the Numbers', *Media Matters for America,* 6 August 2019, https://www.mediamatters.org/fox-news/fox-news-invasion-rhetoric-numbers.

175. Rep. Matt Gaetz, Twitter, 13 July 2020, https://twitter.com/repmattgaetz/status/1282320656500174848.

176. Robert Pape, 'Why We Cannot Afford to Ignore the American Insurrectionist Movement', Chicago Project on Security and Threats, 6 August 2021, https://cpost.uchicago.edu/research/domestic_extremism/why_we_cannot_afford_to_ignore_the_american_insurrectionist_movement/.

177. Ibid.

178. Anita Snow, '1 in 3 Fears Immigrants Influence US Elections: AP-NORC Poll', AP News, 10 May 2022, https://apnews.com/article/immigration-2022-midterm-elections-covid-health-media-2ebbd3849ca35ec76f0f91120639d9d4.

179. Davey and Ebner, 'The Great Replacement'.

180. Ibid.

181. Arnon Grunberg, 'Superhumans, Scapegoats and the Far Right: Busting the Myth of Europe's 'Migrant Crisis'', *Haaretz*, 2 January 2022, https://www.haaretz.com/world-news/.premium-superhumans-scapegoats-and-the-far-right-the-myth-of-europe-s-migrant-crisis-1.10494784.

182. Richard Alba, Morris Levy and Dowell Myers, 'The Myth of a Majority-Minority America', *The Atlantic*, 13 June 2021, https://www.theatlantic.com/ideas/archive/2021/06/myth-majority-minority-america/619190/.

183. Tarrant, 'The Great Replacement'.

184. Itay Lotem, 'A Decade after the Riots, France has Rewritten Its Colonial History', *The Conversation*, 25 January 2016, https://theconversation.com/a-decade-after-the-riots-france-has-rewritten-its-colonial-history-50499.

185. Kyaw Ye Lynn, 'Census Data Shows Myanmar Muslim Population has Fallen', Anadolu Agency, 21 July 2016, https://www.aa.com.tr/en/asia-pacific/census-data-shows-myanmar-muslim-population-has-fallen/612764.

186. 'Buddhism and State Power in Myanmar,' Asia Report 290, International Crisis Group, 5 September 2017, https://www.crisisgroup.org/asia/south-east-asia/myanmar/290-buddhism-and-state-power-myanmar.

187. '969 Movement', https://969movement.org.

188. Gerard McCarthy and Jacqueline Menager, 'Gendered Rumours and the Muslim Scapegoat in Myanmar's Transition', *Journal of Contemporary Asia*, 47, No.3, (2017) 396-412, https://www.tandfonline.com/doi/full/10.1080/00472336.2017.1304563.

189. D. B. Subedi and Johanna Garnett, 'De-mystifying Buddhist Religious Extremism in Myanmar: Confrontation and Contestation around Religion, Development and State-Building', *Conflict, Security & Development*, 20, No.2, (2020), 223–246, https://www.tandfonline.com/doi/full/10.1080/14678802.2020.1739859.

190. Htet Naing Zaw, 'Ma Ba Tha is a Necessity: Military', *The Irrawaddy*, 19 June 2019, https://www.irrawaddy.com/news/burma/ma-ba-tha-necessity-military.html.

191. 'Buddhism and State Power in Myanmar', International Crisis Group.

192. Ibid.

193. Lydia Khalil, 'The Rohingya Tragedy: Time to Talk to the Tatmadaw', *The Interpreter*, 8 March 2017, https://www.lowyinstitute.org/the-interpreter/rohingya-tragedy-time-talk-tatmadaw.

194. Report of the Independent International Fact-Finding Mission, Human Rights Council, HRC/39/64, 12 September 2018, https://www.ohchr.org/Documents/HRBodies/HRCouncil/FFM-Myanmar/A_HRC_39_64.pdf.

195. Ibid.

196. Munira Mustaffa, 'Right-Wing Extremism has Deep Roots in Southeast Asia', *GNET Insights,* 14 July 2021, https://gnet-research.org/2021/07/14/right-wing-extremism-has-deep-roots-in-southeast-asia/.

197. Paul Fuller, 'Myanmar and Buddhist Extremism', *The Conversation,* 15 November 2017, https://theconversation.com/myanmar-and-buddhist-extremism-86125.

198. Hannah Beech, 'The Face of Buddhist Terror,' *Time Magazine,* July 1, 2013, http://content.time.com/time/subscriber/article/0,33009,2146000,00.html.

199. Amresh Gunasingham, 'Buddhist Extremism in Sri Lanka and Myanmar: An Examination.' *Counter Terrorist Trends and Analyses* 11, no. 3 (2019): 1–6. https://www.jstor.org/stable/26617827.

200. Hannah Beech, 'The Face of Buddhist Terror', *Time,* 1 July 2013, http://content.time.com/time/subscriber/article/0,33009,2146000,00.html.

201. Ibid.

202. US Department of State, Office of International Religious Freedom, *2019 Report on International Religious Freedom: Sri Lanka,* (Washington, DC: US Department of State, Office of International Religious Freedom, 2019), https://www.state.gov/reports/2019-report-on-international-religious-freedom/sri-lanka/.

203. Kumar Ramakrishna, 'Deconstructing Buddhist Extremism: Lessons from Sri Lanka', *Religions*, 12, No.11, (2021): 970, https://www.mdpi.com/2077-1444/12/11/970.

204. US Department of State, *2019 Report on International Religious Freedom: Sri Lanka*.

205. Alan Keenan, '"One Country, One Law": The Sri Lankan State's Hostility toward Muslims Grows Deeper', International Crisis Group, Commentary, 23 December 2021, https://www.crisisgroup.org/asia/south-asia/sri-lanka/%E2%80%9Cone-country-one-law%E2%80%9D-sri-lankan-states-hostility-toward-muslims-grows-deeper.

206. Eviane Leidig, 'Hindutva as a Variant of Right-Wing Extremism', *Patterns of Prejudice*, 54, No.3, (2020) 215–237, https://www.tandfonline.com/doi/full/10.1080/0031322X.2020.1759861.

207. Khushwant Singh, *The End of India*, (Penguin, 2003).

208. Madhav Sadashiv Golwalkar, *We or Our Nationhood Defined* (Nagpur: Bharat, 1939), quoted in Leidig, 'Hindutva as a Variant of Right-Wing Extremism'.

209. Marzia Casolari. 'Hindutva's Foreign Tie-Up in the 1930s: Archival Evidence', *Economic and Political Weekly*, 35, No.4 (2000): 218–28, http://www.jstor.org/stable/4408848.

210. Leidig, 'Hindutva as a Variant of Right-Wing Extremism'.

211. Lauren Frayer, 'Nearly 27 Years after Hindu Mob Destroyed Mosque, the Scars in India Remain Deep', National Public Radio, 25 April 2019, https://www.npr.org/2019/04/25/711412924/nearly-27-years-after-hindu-mob-destroyed-a-mosque-the-scars-in-india-remain-dee.

212. 'A Midnight Meeting on Feb 27 and a Murdered Minister', *Outlook*, 5 February 2022, https://www.outlookindia.com/magazine/story/a-midnight-meeting-on-feb-27-and-a-murdered-minister/235982.

213. Dexter Filkins, 'Blood and Soil in Narendra Modi's India', *The New Yorker*, 2 December 2019, https://www.newyorker.com/magazine/2019/12/09/blood-and-soil-in-narendra-modis-india.

214. Hannah Ellis-Petersen and Ahmer Khan, '"They Cut Him into Pieces": India's "Love Jihad" Conspiracy Theory Turns Lethal', *The Guardian*, 21 January 2022, https://www.theguardian.com/world/2022/jan/21/they-cut-him-into-pieces-indias-love-jihad-conspiracy-theory-turns-lethal.

215. Ibid.

216. Leidig, 'Hindutva as a Variant of Right-Wing Extremism'.

217. Repucci and Slipowitz, 'Democracy under Siege'.

218. Emily Schmall and Sameer Yasir, '"Are We Human?" Modi's Use of Antiterror Law Draws Scrutiny from Courts', *The New York Times*, 12 October 2021, https://www.nytimes.com/2021/10/12/world/asia/modi-india-antiterror-law.html.

219. Filkins, 'Blood and Soil in Narendra Modi's India'.

220. Leidig, 'Hindutva as a Variant of Right-Wing Extremism'.

221. 'Expert Warns of Impending 'Genocide' of Muslims in India', Al Jazeera, 16 January 2022, https://www.aljazeera.com/news/2022/1/16/expert-warns-of-possible-genocide-against-muslims-in-india.

222. Anagha Subhash Nair and Ananta Agarwal, 'Hindu Extremists in India Escalate Rhetoric with Calls to Kill Muslims', NBC News, 18 January 2022, https://www.nbcnews.com/news/world/hindu-extremists-india-escalate-rhetoric-calls-kill-muslims-rcna12450.

223. Anders Behring Breivik, '2083: A European Declaration of Independence', 22 July 2011.

224. 'British Far-Right Adopts Indian Hate Campaign Blaming Muslims for Coronavirus', Center for Countering Digital Hate Blog, 1 April 2020, https://counterhate.com/blog/british-far-right-adopts-indian-hate-campaign-blaming-muslims-for-coronavirus/.

225. Ibid.

226. Eviane Leidig, 'The Far-Right is Going Global', *Foreign Policy*, 21 January 2020, https://foreignpolicy.com/2020/01/21/india-kashmir-modi-eu-hindu-nationalists-rss-the-far-right-is-going-global/.

227. Johannes Dafinger and Moritz Florin (eds), *A Transnational History of Right-Wing Terrorism: Political Violence and the Far Right in Eastern and Western Europe Since 1990* (Routledge, 2022).

228. In the manifesto of Dylann Roof, a white supremacist who attacked a Black church in 2015 killing nine people, he wrote that he had 'great respect for the East Asian races ... who are by nature very racist' and could be 'great allies' of whites.

229. 'Violent Right-Wing Extremism and Terrorism – Transnational Connectivity, Definitions, Incidents, Structures and Countermeasures', *Counter Extremism Project*, November 2020, https://www. counterextremism.com/sites/default/files/CEP%20 Study_Violent%20Right-Wing%20Extremism%20 and%20Terrorism_Nov%202020.pdf.

230. Ibid.

231. Kai Bierman et al, 'The Brown Internationale', *Zeit Online*, 11 February 2021, https://www.zeit.de/ gesellschaft/zeitgeschehen/2021-02/fascism-international-right-wing-extremism-neo-nazis-english/seite-2.

232. Perry Barbara and Ryan Scrivens, 'White Pride Worldwide: Constructing Global Identities Online', in *The Globalization of Hate: Internationalizing Hate Crime?* (Oxford: Oxford University Press, 2016).

233. Yassin Musharbash, 'The Globalization of Far-Right Extremism: Investigative Report', *CTC Sentinel*, July/August 2021, https://ctc.usma.edu/the-globalization-of-far-right-extremism-an-investigative-report/.

234. Karim Zidan, 'RAM's Revival and the Ongoing Struggle against MMA's Far-Right Fight Clubs', *The Guardian*, 27 November 2019, https://www.theguardian.com/ sport/2019/nov/27/rams-revival-and-the-ongoing-struggle-against-mmas-far-right-fight-clubs.

235. Tim Hume and Tom Bennett, 'Neo-Nazi Fight Clubs: How the Far-Right Uses MMA to Spread Hate', *Vice News,* 2 November 2021, https://www.vice.com/en/article/7kbpxq/neo-nazi-fight-clubs-how-the-far-right-uses-mma-to-spread-hate.

236. 'Inside a Neo Nazi Music Festival: Decade of Hate', Vice, 19 September 2021, https://www.youtube.com/watch?v=zKX9OjNy_NI.

237. Ibid.

238. Jacob Davey, 'Global Perspectives on the Transnational Far-Right Online Connections', Conference presentation at the RUSI Global Perspectives on the Transnational Far-Right Threat and Response, 3 November 2021, https://rusi.org/events/conferences/global-perspectives-transnational-far-right-threat-and-response/session-two-online-connections.

239. Ibid.

240. Isaac Stanley-Becker, James McAuley and Rick Noack, 'Hesitant Reaction to Charlottesville Spotlights Divisions Within Europe's Far Right', *Washington Post,* 15 August 2017, https://www.washingtonpost.com/world/europe/hesitant-reaction-to-charlottesville-spotlights-divisions-within-europes-far-right/2017/08/15/517fba4e-812a-11e7-9e7a-20fa8d7a0db6_story.html.

241. Katrin Bennhold and Michael Schwirtz, 'Capitol Riot Puts Spotlight on 'Apocalyptically Minded' Global Far Right', *The New York Times,* 14 January 2021, https://www.nytimes.com/2021/01/24/world/europe/capitol-far-right-global.html.

242. 'Violent Right-Wing Extremism and Terrorism – Transnational Connectivity, Definitions, Incidents, Structures and Countermeasures'.

243. Some of the groups referred to here, such as The Base and Atomwaffen Division (now known as NSO), have broken apart and/or reconfigured organisationally.

244. Alex Newhouse, 'The Threat is the Network: The Multi-Node Structure of Neo-Fascist Accelerationism', *CTC Sentinel*, June 2021, https://ctc.usma.edu/the-threat-is-the-network-the-multi-node-structure-of-neo-fascist-accelerationism/.

245. Samantha Springer, 'Secret Tapes Show Neo-Nazi Group The Base Recruiting Former Members of the Military', NBC News, 15 October 2020, https://www.nbcnews.com/news/us-news/secret-tapes-show-neo-nazi-group-base-recruiting-former-members-n1243395.

246. Bierman et al, 'The Brown Internationale'.

247. Southern Poverty Law Center, 'Atomwaffen Division', https://www.splcenter.org/fighting-hate/extremist-files/group/atomwaffen-division.

248. Bierman et al, 'The Brown Internationale'.

249. Fredrik Vejdeland, 'A Strong Minority Trumps a Weak Majority', Nordic Resistance Movement, 5 September 2021, https://nordicresistancemovement.org/a-strong-minority-trumps-a-weak-majority/.

250. 'The Swedish Defence University: 'Transnational Connections Strengthen the Resistance Movement",

Nordic Resistance Movement, 20 September 2021, https://nordicresistancemovement.org/the-swedish-defence-university-transnational-connections-strengthen-the-resistance-movement/.

251. 'Honouring Fallen Comrades from Golden Dawn', Nordic Resistance Movement, 6 November 2018, https://nordicresistancemovement.org/honouring-the-fallen-comrades-from-golden-dawn/.

252. 'The Swedish Defence University: 'Transnational Connections Strengthen the Resistance Movement".

253. 'Violent Right-Wing Extremism and Terrorism – Transnational Connectivity, Definitions, Incidents, Structures and Countermeasures'.

254. Ibid.

255. Stanley-Becker, McAuley and Noack, 'Hesitant Reaction to Charlottesville Spotlights Divisions within Europe's Far Right'.

256. Alan Feuer and Andrew Higgins, 'Extremists Turn to a Leader to Protect Western Values: Vladimir Putin', *The New York Times*, 3 December 2016, https://www.nytimes.com/2016/12/03/world/americas/alt-right-vladimir-putin.html.

257. Anton Troianovski, 'Putin Announces a 'Military Operation' in Ukraine as the UN Security Council Pleads with Him to Pull Back', *The New York Times*, 23 February 2022, https://www.nytimes.com/2022/02/23/world/europe/putin-announces-a-military-operation-in-ukraine-as-the-un-security-council-pleads-with-him-to-pull-back.html.

258. Shelby Butt and Daniel Byman, 'Right-Wing Extremism: The Russian Connection', *Survival*, 62: No.2 (2020) 137–152, https://www.tandfonline.com/doi/full/10.1080/00396338.2020.1739960.

259. Ibid.

260. Steven Erlanger, 'Putin's War on Ukraine is About Ethnicity and Empire', *The New York Times*, 16 March 2022, https://www.nytimes.com/2022/03/16/world/europe/putin-war-ukraine-recolonization.html?referringSource=articleShare.

261. Ibid.

262. Feuer and Higgins. 'Extremists Turn to a Leader to Protect Western Values: Vladimir Putin'.

263. Sarah Riccardi-Swartz, *Between Heaven and Russia: Religious Conversion and Political Apostasy in Appalachia*, first edition, (Fordham University Press, 2022).

264. Y. A. Lyubomirsky, Chairman of the Committee of the World National Conservative Movement, to Jim Dowson, Chairman of the UK Life League, 27 July 2015, St Petersburg, Russia, http://anton-shekhovtsov.blogspot.com/2015/09/russian-politicians-building.html.

265. 'Participants Who are Invited to Participation in 'The World Wide Conservative Movement", World National Conservative Movement memo, undated, https://www.sova-center.ru/files/xeno/parties.pdf.

266. Casey Michel, 'Russian, American White Nationalists Raise Their Flags in Washington', Think Progress, 22 September 2017, https://thinkprogress.org/russian-american-nationalists-washington-5bd15fd18eaf/.

267. Robyn Dixon, 'Inside White-Supremacist Russian Imperial Movement, Designated Foreign Terrorist Organization by the US State Department', *The Washington Post,* 13 April 2020, https://www.washingtonpost.com/world/europe/russia-white-supremacist-terrorism-us/2020/04/11/255a9762-7a75-11ea-a311-adb1344719a9_story.html.

268. Kyle Wilson, 'The Strange Case of Putin's Self-Declared Fifth Column in Australia', *Inside Story,* 12 August 2020, https://insidestory.org.au/the-strange-case-of-putins-self-declared-fifth-column-in-australia/.

269. Nino Bucci, 'Five Australians Free to Return after Fighting in Ukraine Far-Right 'Finishing School' alongside Russian Nationalist Militia', ABC News, 23 April 2019, https://www.abc.net.au/news/2019-04-23/five-australians-free-to-return-after-ukraine-conflict/11004438.

270. Ibid.

271. Alex Man and Kevin Nguyen, 'The Base Tapes', ABC Background Briefing, 26 March 2021, https://www.abc.net.au/news/2021-03-26/the-base-tapes-secret-recordings-australian-recruitment/13255994.

272. The Honourable Karen Andrews, Minister for Home Affairs, 'Morrison Government to List Two New Terrorist Organisations', Media Release, 24 November 2021, https://minister.homeaffairs.gov.au/KarenAndrews/Pages/morrison-government-list-two-new-terrorist-organisations.aspx.

273. Ahmed Rashid, *Taliban: Militant Islam, Oil and Fundamentalism in Central Asia*, (New Haven: Yale University Press, 2010).

274. Muhammad Haniff Hassan, 'Mobilization of Muslims for Jihad: Insights from the Past and Their Relevance Today', *Counter Terrorist Trends and Analyses* Vol. 5, No.8 (2013): 10–15. http://www.jstor.org/stable/26351173.

275. Fawaz Gerges, *The Far Enemy: Why Jihad Went Global*, (Cambridge: Cambridge University Press, 2009).

276. Musharbash, 'The Globalization of Far-Right Extremism: Investigative Report'.

277. Egle Murauskaite, 'Foreign Fighters in Ukraine: Assessing Potential Risks', Vilnius Institute for Policy Analysis, 2020, https://vilniusinstitute.lt/wp-content/uploads/2020/02/FOREIGN-FIGHTERS-IN-UKRAINE-ASSESSING-POTENTIAL-RISKS.pdf.

278. Kacper Rekawek, 'Career Break or a New Career? Extremist Foreign Fighters in Ukraine', Counter Extremism Project, April 2020, https://www.counterextremism.com/sites/default/files/CEP%20Report_Career%20Break%20or%20a%20New%20Career_Extremist%20Foreign%20Fighters%20in%20Ukraine_April%202020.pdf.

279. Ibid.

280. Ibid.

281. Ibid.

282. Ibid.

283. Murauskaite, 'Foreign Fighters in Ukraine: Assessing Potential Risks'.

284. Roman Goncharenko, 'The Azov Battalion: Extremists Defending Mariupol, DW, 16 March 2022, https://www.dw.com/en/the-azov-battalion-extremists-defending-mariupol/a-61151151.

285. 'Who are Ukraine's Far-Right Azov Regiment?', Al Jazeera, 1 March 2022, https://www.aljazeera.com/news/2022/3/1/who-are-the-azov-regiment.

286. Simon Shuster and Billy Perrigo, 'Like, Share, Recruit: How a Supremacist Militia Uses Facebook to Radicalize and Train New Members', *Time*, 7 January 2021, https://time.com/5926750/azov-far-right-movement-facebook/.

287. 'Report on the Human Rights Situation in Ukraine, 16 February to 15 May 2016', United Nations Human Rights, Office of the High Commissioner, https://www.ohchr.org/Documents/Countries/UA/Ukraine_14th_HRMMU_Report.pdf.

288. 'White Supremacy Extremism: The Transnational Rise of the Violent White Supremacist Movement', The Soufan Center, September 2019, https://thesoufancenter.org/wp-content/uploads/2019/09/Report-by-The-Soufan-Center-White-Supremacy-Extremism-The-Transnational-Rise-of-The-Violent-White-Supremacist-Movement.pdf.

289. Shuster and Perrigo, 'Like, Share, Recruit'.

290. Oleksiy Kuzmenko, '"Defend the White Race": American Extremists Being Co-opted by Ukraine's Far-Right', Bellingcat, 15 February 2019,

https://www.bellingcat.com/news/uk-and-europe/2019/02/15/defend-the-white-race-american-extremists-being-co-opted-by-ukraines-far-right/.

291. Paul Osborne, 'Fears of Ukraine Drawing Foreign Fighters', Seven News, 10 February 2022, https://7news.com.au/politics/fears-of-ukraine-drawing-foreign-fighters-c-5638472.

292. Sean Rubinsztein-Dunlop, Suzanne Dredge and Michael Workman, 'From Neo-Nazi to Militant: The Foreign Fighters in Ukraine who Australia's Laws Won't Stop', ABC News, 1 May 2018, https://www.abc.net.au/news/2018-05-01/foreign-fighters-return-to-australia- with-military-training/9696784.

293. Bucci, 'Five Australians Free to Return After Fighting in Ukraine Far-Right 'Finishing School' Alongside Russian Nationalist Militia'.

294. Ibid.

295. Parliament of the Commonwealth of Australia, 'Review of the Declared Area Provisions, Sections 119.2 and 119.3 of the Criminal Code', Parliamentary Joint Committee on Intelligence and Security, February 2018, Canberra, Commonwealth of Australia, https://www.aph.gov.au/Parliamentary_Business/Committees/Joint/Intelligence_and_Security/DeclaredArea/Report/section?id=committees%2Freportjnt%2F024117%2F25400.

296. Liam Mendes, 'Australians can go Fight for Either Side in Ukraine-Russia Conflict', The Australian, 27 February 2022, https://www.theaustralian.com.au/world/australians-can-go-fight-for-either-side-in-ukrainerussia-conflict/news-story/9bb11aa6aad5c50b23958c645b868d8a.

297. Murauskaite, 'Foreign Fighters in Ukraine: Assessing Potential Risks'.

298. Kuzmenko, '"Defend the White Race": American Extremists Being Co-opted by Ukraine's Far-Right'.

299. Christopher Miller, 'Azov, Ukraine's Most Prominent Ultranationalist Group, Set Its Sights on US, Europe', *Radio Free Europe*, 14 November 2018, https://www.rferl.org/a/azov-ukraine-s-most-prominent-ultranationalist-group-sets-its-sights-on-u-s-europe/29600564.html.

300. Weiyi Cai and Simone Landon, 'Attacks by White Extremists Are Growing. So Are Their Connections', *New York Times*, 3 April 2019, https://www.nytimes.com/interactive/2019/04/03/world/white-extremist-terrorism-christchurch.html.

301. '"We're Just Mums and Dads": Inside Reclaim Australia', Yahoo News, 12 October 2015, https://au.news.yahoo.com/were-just-mums-and-dads-inside-reclaim-australia-29784783.html.

302. Joey Watson, 'Everyone Wants to Be Fuhrer', *Earshot*, Radio National, 14 March 2022, https://www.abc.net.au/radionational/programs/earshot/everyone-wants-to-be-fuhrer-1/13774644.

303. Alex Mann and Kevin Nguyen, 'Former New Guard Insider Reveals Neo-Nazi Group's Recruitment Tactics', ABC Background Briefing, 2 April 2021, https://www.abc.net.au/news/2021-04-02/insider-shares-neo-nazi-group-s-recruitment-tactics/100040822.

304. Joey Watson, 'Everyone Wants to Be Fuhrer', *Earshot*, Radio National, 14 March 2022, https://www.abc.net.au/radionational/programs/earshot/everyone-wants-to-be-fuhrer-1/13774644.

305. Charlie Winter et al, 'Online Extremism: Research Trends in Internet Activism, Radicalization, and Counter-Strategies', *International Journal of Conflict and Violence,* vol. 14, no.2: (2020) 1–20.

306. Cai and Landon, 'Attacks by White Extremists Are Growing. So Are Their Connections'.

307. Maura Conway, Ryan Scrivens and Logan Macnair, 'Right-Wing Extremists' Persistent Online Presence: History and Contemporary Trends', ICCT, Policy Brief, October 2019, https://icct.nl/app/uploads/2019/11/Right-Wing-Extremists-Persistent-Online-Presence.pdf.

308. Laura Smith, 'Lone Wolves Connected Online: A History of Modern White Supremacy', *The New York Times,* 26 January 2021, https://www.nytimes.com/2021/01/26/us/louis-beam-white-supremacy-internet.html.

309. Lynne Ianniello, Anti-Defamation League press release, 1985, https://ia800203.us.archive.org/13/items/ComputerizedNetworksOfHate/ADL_news_release.pdf.

310. Joey Watson, 'Everyone Wants to Be Fuhrer', *Earshot*, ABC Radio National, 14 March 2022, https://www.abc.net.au/radionational/programs/earshot/everyone-wants-to-be-fuhrer-ep-2/13785880.

311. Thomas Hegghammer, *Jihadi Culture: The Art and Social Practices of Militant Islamists*, (Cambridge: Cambridge University Press, 2017).

312. Pete Lentini, 'The Transference of Neojihadism: Towards a Process Theory of Transnational Radicalisation', *Radicalisation Crossing Borders: New Directions in Islamist and Jihadist Political, Intellectual and Theological Thought in Practice*, Global Terrorism Research Centre, Monash University, 2009, 26–27, https://www.monash.edu/__data/assets/pdf_file/0004/1677640/gtrec-proceedings-2008-01-pete-lentini.pdf.

313. Anna Kelsey-Sugg and Siobhan Marin, 'For Some, being a Tradwife is about More Time with Family. For Others, It's a Dangerous Far-Right Ideology', *This Much is True*, ABC News, 22 August 2021, https://www.abc.net.au/news/2021-08-22/tradwife-movement-personal-pleasures-or-extreme-right-ideologies/100356514.

314. Caitlin Dewy, 'Absolutely Everything You Need to Know to Understand 4chan, the Internet's Own Bogeyman', *The Washington Post*, 25 September 2014, https://www.washingtonpost.com/news/the-intersect/wp/2014/09/25/absolutely-everything-you-need-to-know-to-understand-4chan-the-internets-own-bogeyman/.

315. Matthew Prince, 'Terminating Service for 8chan', *Cloudfare Blog*, 8 May 2019, https://blog.cloudflare.com/terminating-service-for-8chan/.

316. Conway, Scrivens and Macnair, 'Right-Wing Extremists' Persistent Online Presence: History and Contemporary Trends'.

317. Cathrine Thorleifsson and Joey Duker, 'Lone Actors in Digital Environments', Radicalisation Awareness Network Report (European Commission: 2021), https://ec.europa.eu/home-affairs/system/files/2021-10/ran_paper_lone_actors_in_digital_environments_en.pdf.

318. A type of artefact or cultural unit of meaning, usually an image with text that provides a commentary on culture, ideas or current events that are humorous or ironic.

319. Whitney Phillips and Ryan Milner, *The Ambivalent Internet: Mischief, Oddity and Antagonism Online*, (Polity, 2017).

320. Morgan Sung, '4chan Trolling Turned the OK Sign into a Symbol of Hate', *Mashable,* 26 September 2019, https://mashable.com/article/ok-hand-gesture-hate-symbol-anti-defamation-league-white-sumpremacy.

321. 'Okay Hand Gesture', Hate on Display Guide, Anti-Defamation League, https://www.adl.org/education/references/hate-symbols/okay-hand-gesture.

322. Helen Lewis, 'The Joke's on Us', *The Atlantic,* 30 September 2022, https://www.theatlantic.com/international/archive/2020/09/how-memes-lulz-and-ironic-bigotry-won-internet/616427/.

323. Lisa Bogerts and Maik Fielitz, 'The Visual Culture of Far-Right Terrorism', *PRIF Blog,* 31 March 2020, https://blog.prif.org/2020/03/31/the-visual-culture-of-far-right-terrorism/.

324. Maik Fielitz and Reem Ahmed, 'It's Not Funny Anymore. Far-Right Extremists' Use of Humour', Radicalisation Awareness Network Report (European Commission: 2021), https://ec.europa.eu/home-affairs/system/files/2021-03/ran_ad-hoc_pap_fre_humor_20210215_en.pdf.

325. Ashley Feinburg, 'This is Daily Stormer's Playbook', *Huffington Post,* 3 December 2017, https://www.huffingtonpost.co.uk/entry/daily-stormer-nazi-style-guide_n_5a2ece19e4b0ce3b344492f2?ri18n=true.

326. Ibid.

327. Ibid.

328. Bogerts and Fielitz, 'The Visual Culture of Far-Right Terrorism'.

329. Robert Evans, 'Shitposting, Inspirational Terrorism and the Christchurch Mosque Massacre', Bellingcat, 15 March 2019, https://www.bellingcat.com/news/rest-of-world/2019/03/15/shitposting-inspirational-terrorism-and-the-christchurch-mosque-massacre/.

330. Bart Schuurman, et al, 'End of the Lone Wolf: The Typology that Should Never have been', *Studies in Conflict & Terrorism*, 42, No.8 (2019), 771–778.

331. As quoted in, Nicky Woolf, 'Destroyer of Worlds', Tortoise Media, 29 June 2019, https://www.tortoisemedia.com/2019/06/29/8chan/.

332. Fielitz and Ahmed, 'It's Not Funny Anymore. Far-Right Extremists' use of Humour'.

333. Royal Commission of Inquiry into the Terrorist Attack on the Christchurch Mosques on 15 March 2019, Part 4, Chapter 3, 21 December 2020, https://christchurchattack.royalcommission.nz/the-report/firearms-licensing/the-regulation-of-semi-automatic-firearms/.

334. Ibid.

335. Cai and Landon, 'Attacks by White Extremists are Growing. So are Their Connections'.

336. Graham Macklin, 'The El Paso Terrorist Attack: The Chain Reaction of Global Right-Wing Terror', *CTC Sentinel,* 12, No.11 (December 2019), https://ctc.usma.edu/el-paso-terrorist-attack-chain-reaction-global-right-wing-terror/.

337. J. M. Berger, 'The Strategy of Violent White Supremacy is Evolving', *The Atlantic,* 8 August 2019, https://www.theatlantic.com/ideas/archive/2019/08/the-new-strategy-of-violent-white-supremacy/595648/.

338. 'The Russians and Ukrainians Translating the Christchurch Shooter's Manifesto', Bellingcat, 14 August 2019, https://www.bellingcat.com/news/uk-and-europe/2019/08/14/the-russians-and-ukrainians-translating-the-christchurch-shooters-manifesto/.

339. Evans, 'Shitposting, Inspirational Terrorism and the Christchurch Mosque Massacre'.

340. Jason Burke, 'Norway Mosque Attack Suspect "Inspired by Christchurch and El Paso Shootings"',

The Guardian, 12 August 2019, https://www. theguardian.com/world/2019/aug/11/norway- mosque-attack-suspect-may-have-been-inspired-by- christchurch-and-el-paso-shootings.

341. Thorleifsson and Duker, 'Lone Actors in Digital Environments'.

342. Sebastian Deterding et al, 'From Game Design Elements to Gamefulness: Defining Gamification', MindTrek '11: Proceedings of the 15th International Academic MindTrek Conference: Envisioning Future Media Environments, September 2011, 9–15, https:// doi.org/10.1145/2181037.2181040.

343. Linda Schlegel, 'Jumanji Extremism? How Games and Gamification Could Facilitate Radicalization Processes', *Journal for Deradicalization,* Summer, No.23 (June 2020), https://journals.sfu.ca/jd/index. php/jd/article/view/359/223.

344. Graham Macklin, 'The Christchurch Attacks: Livestream Terror in the Viral Video Age', CTC Sentinel, Vol.12, No.6 (July 2109), https://ctc.usma. edu/christchurch-attacks-livestream-terror-viral- video-age/.

345. As quoted in Macklin, 'The El Paso Terrorist Attack: The Chain Reaction of Global Right-Wing Terror'.

346. Smith, 'Lone Wolves Connected Online: A History of Modern White Supremacy'.

347. J. M. Berger, 'The Turner Legacy: The Storied Origins and Enduring Impact of White Nationalism's Deadly

Bible', ICCT Research Paper, September 2016, https://
icct.nl/app/uploads/2016/09/ICCT-Berger-The-Turner-
Legacy-September2016-2.pdf.

348. Andrew MacDonald (pseudonym of William Luther
Pierce), *The Turner Diaries*, (Washington, DC:
National Vanguard Books, 1978).

349. Alexandra Alter, 'How 'The Turner Diaries' Incites
White Supremacists', *The New York Times*,
12 January 2021, https://www.nytimes.com/2021/01/12/
books/turner-diaries-white-supremacists.html.

350. Berger, 'The Turner Legacy: The Storied Origins
and Enduring Impact of White Nationalism's Deadly
Bible'.

351. Jacob Ware, 'Siege: The Atomwaffen Division and
Rising Far-Right Terrorism in the United States',
ICCT Policy Brief, July 2019, https://icct.nl/app/
uploads/2019/07/ICCT-Ware-Siege-July2019.pdf.

352. Louis Beam, 'Leaderless Resistance', *The Seditionist*,
12 February 1992.

353. James Mason, 'Later on We'll Conspire', September
1980, in *Siege*, 3rd edition (IronMarch.org Publication,
2017).

354. Jan-Willem van Prooijen and Nils B. Jostmann, 'Belief
in Conspiracy Theories: The Influence of Uncertainty
and Perceived Morality', *European Journal of Social
Psychology*, 43, No.1 (December, 2012), 109–115,
https://doi.org/10.1002/ejsp.1922.

355. Kate Cox, et al, 'Covid-19, Disinformation and Online Extremism', Literature Review Report Prepared for the Commission for Countering Extremism (CCE), March 2021, https://assets.publishing.service.gov.uk/government/uploads/system/uploads/attachment_data/file/993842/RAND_Europe_Final_Report_Hateful_Extremism_During_COVID-19_Final.pdf.

356. Michael Barkun, *Disaster and the Millennium,* (New Haven: Yale University Press, 1974).

357. 'City Locked Down for Three Months has Bleak Lessons for the World', Bloomberg, 28 October 2020, https://www.bloomberg.com/news/articles/2020-10-28/city-locked-down-for-three-months-has-bleak-lesson-for-the-world.

358. Anthony Piovesan and Rhiannon Tuffield, 'Counter-Terrorism Police Charge Melbourne Man after Alleged Daniel Andrews Death Threat', News.com.au, 18 November 2021, https://www.news.com.au/national/victoria/news/counterterrorism-police-charge-melbourne-man-after-alleged-daniel-andrews-death-threat/news-story/eff00cdacad248bbd388e704ebf90f87.

359. Mariam Kiparoidze, 'QAnon Followers Think Trump will be back in the White House by March', *.coda,* 29 January 2021, https://www.codastory.com/disinformation/qanon-sovereign-citizen/.

360. Zac Crellin, 'From Anti-Vaxxers to 'Sovereign Citizens': A Who's Who of the Convoy to Canberra Protest', *The New Daily,* 7 February 2022, https://thenewdaily.com.au/news/national/2022/02/07/canberra-protest-anti-vaxxers/.

361. Blake Foden, 'Convoy to Canberra Protest Leader James Greer Granted Bail on Firearms, Ammunition Charge', *Canberra Times*, 5 February 2022, https://www.canberratimes.com.au/story/7608345/anti-vax-leader-bailed-after-rifle-124-rounds-allegedly-found-in-truck/.

362. Cloe Read, 'Man Charged after AFP Commissioner Impersonated in Alleged Plot to Overthrow Government', *The Sydney Morning Herald*, 2 August 2021, https://www.smh.com.au/politics/federal/man-charged-after-afp-commissioner-impersonated-in-alleged-plot-to-overthrow-government-20210802-p58f8r.html.

363. Jack Latimore, '"Blackfishing": Alt-Right Pushes to Co-opt Aboriginal Tent Embassy to Cause', *The Sydney Morning Herald*, 8 January 2022, https://www.smh.com.au/national/anti-lockdown-activists-spreading-dangerous-lies-about-covid-response-in-indigenous-communities-20211125-p59c4z.html.

364. Simone Fox Koob et al, 'Anti-Lockdown Activists Spread Dangerous Lies about Covid Response in Indigenous Communities', *The Sydney Morning Herald*, 25 November 2021, https://www.smh.com.au/national/blackfishing-alt-right-pushes-to-co-opt-aboriginal-tent-embassy-to-cause-20220105-p59lzj.html.

365. Ian Austen and Vjosa Isai, 'Canadian Trucker Convoy Descends on Ottawa to Protest Vaccine Mandates', *The New York Times*, 29 January 2022, https://www.nytimes.com/2022/01/29/world/americas/canada-trucker-protest.html.

366. Jason Horowitz, 'Trucker Protests in Canada: What You Need to Know', *The New York Times,* 20 February 2022, https://www.nytimes.com/2022/01/29/world/americas/canada-trucker-protest.html.

367. Sheera Frenkel, 'Canada Convoy Draws Online Support from Far-Right Activists around the World', *The New York Times,* 7 February 2022, https://www.nytimes.com/2022/01/29/world/americas/canada-trucker-protest.html.

368. Richard Baker et al, '"Freedom" Activists Aim to Harness Anger for New Political Party', *The Sydney Morning Herald,* 31 July 2001, https://www.smh.com.au/national/freedom-activists-aim-to-harness-anger-for-new-political-party-20210730-p58edq.html.

369. Ian Austen, 'Long After Blockade, Canada's Truckers Have a Political Champion', *The New York Times,* 11 May 2022, https://www.nytimes.com/2022/01/29/world/americas/canada-trucker-protest.html.

370. Ed White, 'Informant Provides Key Details about Plot to Kidnap Michigan Gov. Whitmer', PBS News Hour, 18 March 2022, https://www.pbs.org/newshour/politics/informant-provides-key-details-about-plot-to-kidnap-michigan-gov-whitmer.

371. 'San Pedro Train Engineer Pleads Guilty to Terrorism Charge for Intentionally Derailing Locomotive Near US Navy Hospital Ship', Press Release, Department of Justice, US Attorney Office, Central District of California, 16 December 2021, https://www.justice.gov/usao-cdca/pr/san-pedro-train-engineer-pleads-guilty-terrorism-charge-intentionally-derailing.

372. Dan Diamond, 'Fauci Gets Security Detail after Receiving Threats', *Politico*, 1 April 2020, https://www.politico.com/news/2020/04/01/fauci-coronavirus-security-160901.

373. Adam Goldman, 'Man Suspected of Planning Attack on Missouri Hospital is Killed, Officials Say', *The New York Times*, 25 March 2020, https://www.nytimes.com/2020/03/25/us/politics/coronavirus-fbi-shooting.html.

374. 'White Racially Motivated Violent Extremists Suggest Spreading the Coronavirus', US Department of Homeland Security, Federal Protective Service (FPS) Weekly Intelligence Brief, 17–21 February 2020, https://www.scribd.com/document/452676693/White-Supremacist-Corona#fullscreen&from_embed.

375. 'White Supremacists Respond to Coronavirus with Violent Plots and Online Hate', *ADL Blog*, 26 March 2020, https://lasvegas.adl.org/white-supremacists-respond-to-coronavirus-with-violent-plots-and-online-hate/.

376. Lydia Khalil, 2020–2021, 'Crisis Points' research project dataset, unpublished.

377. 'United Nations Guidance Note on Addressing and Countering Covid-19 related Hate Speech', 11 May 2020, https://www.un.org/en/genocideprevention/documents/Guidance%20on%20COVID-19%20related%20Hate%20Speech.pdf.

378. Daveed Gartenstein-Ross et al, 'The Growing Threat Posed by Accelerationism and Accelerationist Groups

Worldwide', Foreign Policy Research Institute Analysis, 20 April 2020, https://www.fpri.org/article/2020/04/the-growing-threat-posed-by-accelerationism-and-accelerationist-groups-worldwide/.

379. Matthew Kriner and Jon Lewis, 'Pride & Prejudice: The Violent Evolution of the Proud Boys', CTC Sentinel, Vol.14, No.6 (July/August 2021), https://ctc.westpoint.edu/pride-prejudice-the-violent-evolution-of-the-proud-boys/.

380. '"You Can't Spot the White Nationalist Anymore": Inside the Rise of Right-Wing Extremism', *Meet the Press*, NBC News, 19 April 2021, https://www.youtube.com/watch?v=FvUibXZWvmY.

381. Wes Mountain, 'Is Sky News Shifting Australian Politics to the Right? Not Yet, but There is Cause for Alarm', *The Conversation*, 22 February 2021, https://theconversation.com/is-sky-news-shifting-australian-politics-to-the-right-not-yet-but-there-is-cause-for-alarm-155356.

382. 'Sky News Admits it was "Wrong" to Air Interview with Cottrell from United Patriots Front', ABC News, 6 August 2018, https://www.abc.net.au/news/2018-08-06/sky-news-apologises-for-airing-interview-with-blair-cottrell/10076074.

383. For example, Lauren Southern is identified as a 'contributor' in this clip: 'Lauren Southern Calls for Next US President to Investigate Tech Giant Censorship', Sky News, 6 November 2020, https://www.skynews.com.au/australia-news/lauren-southern-calls-for-next-us-president-to-investigate-tech-giant-censorship/video/961a9ccb5430ad1122886a2c57b4451b.

384. Amanda Meade, 'Steve Bannon Backlash as Four Corners Interview Splits the ABC', *The Guardian,* 7 September 2018, https://www.theguardian.com/media/commentisfree/2018/sep/07/steve-bannon-backlash-as-four-corners-interview-splits-the-abc.

385. Macquarie University Department of Security Studies, 'Mapping Networks and Narratives of Right-Wing Extremists in New South Wales', Technical Report for Department of Communities and Justice NSW, 2020, https://doi.org/10.5281/ZENODO.4071472.

386. Whitney Phillips, 'The Oxygen of Amplification: Better Practices for Reporting on Extremists, Antagonists, and Manipulators Online', *Data and Society,* https://datasociety.net/wp-content/uploads/2018/05/1_PART_1_Oxygen_of_Amplification_DS.pdf.

387. Ibid.

388. Mario Peucker et al, 'Mapping Networks and Narratives of Far-Right Movements in Victoria', Victoria University Monograph, 2018, https://vuir.vu.edu.au/42464/.

389. Rick Morton, 'Murdoch Media Fuels Far-Right Recruitment', *The Saturday Paper,* 10–16 August 2019, https://www.thesaturdaypaper.com.au/news/politics/2019/08/10/murdoch-media-fuels-far-right-recruitment/15653592008581.

390. Andrew Bolt, 'There is No 'Us', as Migrants Form Colonies', *Herald Sun,* 2 August 2018, https://www.heraldsun.com.au/blogs/andrew-bolt/there-is-no-us-as-migrants-form-colonies/news-story/919f583813314a3a9ec8c4c74bc8c091.

391. Phillips, 'The Oxygen of Amplification: Better Practices for Reporting on Extremists, Antagonists, and Manipulators Online'.

392. Michele Grossman et al, 'The Stocktake Research Project: A Systematic Literature and Selected Program Review on Social Cohesion, Community Resilience and Violent Extremism 2011–2015', Community Resilience Unit, Victorian Department of Premier and Cabinet, Melbourne, Victoria, 2016, https://www.amf.net.au/library/uploads/files/15412_Stocktake_Research_Program_V13_(1).pdf.

393. Phillips, 'The Oxygen of Amplification: Better Practices for Reporting on Extremists, Antagonists, and Manipulators Online'.

394. Derek Thompson, 'Donald Trump is Helping the Very Media Organizations He Despises', *The Atlantic,* 5 May 2017, https://www.theatlantic.com/business/archive/2017/05/donald-trump-media-enemies/525381/.

395. Joe Hagan, '"Dishonesty . . . Is Always an Indicator of Weakness": Tucker Carlson on How He Brought His Coronavirus Message to Mar-a-Lago', *Vanity Fair,* 17 March 2020, https://www.vanityfair.com/news/2020/03/tucker-carlson-on-how-he-brought-coronavirus-message-to-mar-a-lago?cid=eml_dbm_20200911&utm_source=Sailthru&utm_medium=email&utm_campaign=BYERS%20MARKET%202020.09.11&utm_term=Byers%20Market.

396. Patricia Sabga, 'Jeff Zucker, Who Helped Propel Trump to Power, Resigns from CNN', Al Jazeera,

2 February 2022, https://www.aljazeera.com/
economy/2022/2/2/jeff-zucker-who-helped-propel-
trump-to-power-resigns-from-cnn.

397. Dylan Byers and Ahiza Garcia-Hodges, 'Jeff Zucker,
Michael Cohen and the Business of News', *Byers Market,*
11 September 2020, https://link.nbcnews.com/view/
5bce14339c625f4457579519cs9x4.7bo/77b31599.

398. 'Enemies of the People', *Vice News,* Series 1,
Episode 19, https://www.vicetv.com/en_us/video/
enemies-of-the-people/5f80862e3f3b0d76ba7a24f1.

399. Mark Triffitt, 'A Growing Mistrust in Democracy
is Causing Extremism and Strongman Politics to
Flourish', *The Conversation,* 10 July 2018, https://
theconversation.com/a-growing-mistrust-in-democracy-
is-causing-extremism-and-strongman-politics-to-
flourish-98621.

400. Ehud Sprinzak, 'The Process of Delegitimation:
Towards a Linkage Theory of Political Terrorism',
Terrorism and Political Violence, 3, No.1, 50–68.

401. Ronald Reagan for President campaign ad, Reagan
Foundation, 1980, https://www.youtube.com/
watch?v=SBfzwycHOcY.

402. Niskanen Center, 'Did Chinese Trade Competition
Increase Nativism and Elect Trump?', 16 January
2019, https://www.niskanencenter.org/did-chinese-
trade-competition-increase-nativism-and-elect-trump/.

403. Kevin Roose and Ali Winston, 'Far-Right Internet
Groups Listen for Trump's Approval, and Often

Hear It', *The New York Times*, 4 November 2018, https://www.nytimes.com/2018/11/04/us/politics/far-right-internet-trump.html.

404. Bethan Johnson and Matthew Feldman, 'Siege Culture after Siege: Anatomy of a Neo-Nazi Terrorist Doctrine', ICCT Research Paper, July 2021, https://icct.nl/app/uploads/2021/07/siege-culture-neo-nazi-terrorist-doctrine.pdf.

405. Ibid.

406. Lydia Khalil, 'Inciter in Chief', *The Interpreter*, 29 October 2020, https://www.lowyinstitute.org/the-interpreter/inciter-chief.

407. 'President Donald Trump Urges His Supporters: 'Go into the Polls and Watch Very Carefully'', CNBC TV, 30 September 2020, https://www.youtube.com/watch?v=HdECDoioHU0.

408. Jaclyn Diaz and Rachel Treisman, 'Members of Right-Wing Militias, Extremist Groups are Latest Charged in Capitol Siege', NPR News, 19 January 2021, https://www.npr.org/sections/insurrection-at-the-capitol/2021/01/19/958240531/members-of-right-wing-militias-extremist-groups-are-latest-charged-in-capitol-si.

409. Rebecca Boone et al, 'Mix of Extremists who Stormed Capitol isn't Retreating', AP News, 14 January 2021, https://apnews.com/article/capitol-siege-extremist-groups-80e309418abecd0b1d50ec476 2e6d9c6.

410. Hugo Lowell, 'Capitol Attack Panel Investigates Trump over Potential Criminal Conspiracy', *The Guardian,* 8 January 2022, https://www.theguardian.com/us-news/2022/jan/08/capitol-attack-committee-donald-trump-white-house-stop-biden-win.

411. Attachment to Form Answer of Defendant Matthew Heimbach to Complaint of Plaintiffs Kashtya Nwanguma, Molly Shaw and Henry Brousseau, Case 3:16-cv-00247-DJH-HBB, Document 31-2, filed 17 April 2017, https://www.politico.com/f/?id=0000015b-7dcc-db04-ad5b-7ded76a30002.

412. Eric Kleefeld, 'Fox News Says We Should Respond to the January 6 Insurrectionists by Implementing Their Anti-Voting Agenda', *Media Matters,* 8 January 2010, https://www.mediamatters.org/voter-fraud-and-suppression/fox-news-says-we-should-respond-january-6-insurrectionists-implementing.

413. Alan Feuer and Nicole Hong, '"I Answered the Call of My President": Rioters Say Trump Urged Them On', *The New York Times,* 17 January 2021, https://www.nytimes.com/2021/01/17/nyregion/protesters-blaming-trump-pardon.html.

414. Marianna Spring, '"Stop the Steal": The Deep Roots of Trump's 'Voter Fraud' Strategy', BBC News, 23 November 2020, https://www.bbc.com/news/blogs-trending-55009950.

415. Sara Swann, 'No, Most Americans Don't Believe the Vote was Fraudulent,' *Politfact,* 2 February 2022, https://www.politifact.com/factchecks/2022/feb/02/viral-image/no-most-americans-dont-believe-2020-election-was-f/.

416. Glenn Kessler, Salvador Rizzo and Meg Kelly, 'Trump's False or Misleading Claims Total 30,573 over Four Years', *The Washington Post*, 24 January 2021, https://www.washingtonpost.com/politics/2021/01/24/trumps-false-or-misleading-claims-total-30573-over-four-years/.

417. Timothy Snyder, 'The American Abyss: A Historian of Fascism and Political Atrocity on Trump, the Mob and What Comes Next', *The New York Times*, 9 January 2021, https://www.nytimes.com/2021/01/09/magazine/trump-coup.html.

418. Colby Itkowitz, et al, 'Trump Praises Baseless QAnon Conspiracy Theory, Says He Appreciates Support of Its Followers', *The Washington Post*, 19 August 2020, https://www.washingtonpost.com/politics/trump-praises-baseless-qanon-conspiracy-theory-says-he-appreciates-support-of-its-followers/2020/08/19/e50f8d46-e25e-11ea-8181-606e603bb1c4_story.html?itid=lk_inline_manual_40.

419. 'Capitol Riot: 'QAnon Shaman' Jacob Chansley Sentenced to 41 Months in Prison', BBC News, 17 November 2021, https://www.bbc.com/news/world-us-canada-59253090.

420. 'The Persistence of QAnon in the Trump Era: An Analysis of Who Believes the Conspiracies', PRRI, 24 February 2022, https://www.prri.org/research/the-persistence-of-qanon-in-the-post-trump-era-an-analysis-of-who-believes-the-conspiracies/.

421. Alex Kaplan, 'Here are the QAnon Supporters Running for Congress in 2020', Media Matters for

America, 1 January 2020, https://www.mediamatters.org/qanon-conspiracy-theory/here-are-qanon-supporters-running-congress-2020.

422. Joshua Zitser and Sophia Ankel, 'A Trump-Loving Insurrectionist and a Convicted Stalker are among 36 QAnon Supporters Running for Congress in 2022', *Business Insider,* 27 June 2021, https://www.businessinsider.com/the-36-qanon-supporters-running-congress-in-the-2022-midterms-2021-6.

423. Jacob Rosen, et al, 'QAnon Promoter Ron Watkins is Running for Congress in Arizona', CBS News, 29 October 2021, https://www.cbsnews.com/news/qanon-promoter-ron-watkins-is-running-for-congress-in-arizona/.

424. '2021 Far-Right Conferences: QAnon and Other Extremist Ideologies Dominate Events', ADL Report, 2 July 2021, https://www.adl.org/resources/reports/2021-far-right-conferences-qanon-and-other-extremist-ideologies-dominate-events.

425. Jonathan Chait, 'Why Republicans are Smearing Everyone as Pedophiles Now', *New York Magazine,* 5 April 2022, https://nymag.com/intelligencer/2022/04/why-republicans-are-smearing-everyone-as-pedophiles-now.html.

426. Frida Ghitis, 'QAnon is an American Invention, but it has become a Global Plague', *The Washington Post,* 10 March 2021, https://www.washingtonpost.com/opinions/2021/03/10/qanon-japan-germany-colombia-conspiracy-theories-disinformation/.

427. Van Badham, 'QAnon: How the Far-Right Cult Took Australia Down a 'Rabbit Hole' of Extremism', *The Guardian*, 14 November 2021, https://www.theguardian.com/us-news/2021/nov/14/qanon-how-the-far-right-cult-took-australians-down-a-rabbit-hole-of-extremism.

428. Aoife Gallagher, Jacob Davey and Mackenzie Hart, *The Genesis of a Conspiracy Theory: Key Trends in QAnon Activity Since 2017*, (London: Institute for Strategic Dialogue, 2020), https://www.isdglobal.org/wp-content/uploads/2020/07/The-Genesis-of-a-Conspiracy-Theory.pdf.

429. Kristy Campion, 'A 'Lunatic Fringe'? The Persistence of Right-Wing Extremism Australia', *Perspectives on Terrorism*, 13, No.2 (April, 2019), https://www.universiteitleiden.nl/binaries/content/assets/customsites/perspectives-on-terrorism/2019/issue-2/campion.pdf.

430. Macquarie University Department of Security Studies, 'Mapping Networks and Narratives of Right-Wing Extremists in New South Wales', Technical Report for Department of Communities and Justice, NSW, Countering Violent Extremism (CVE) Programs, 2020, https://doi.org/10.5281/ZENODO.4071472.

431. Daniel Hurst and Naaman Zhou, 'Australian Acting PM's 'All Lives Matter' Comment Labelled 'Beyond Disgusting'', *The Guardian*, 12 January 2021, https://www.theguardian.com/australia-news/2021/jan/12/australian-acting-pm-michael-mccormack-all-lives-matter-comment-labelled-beyond-disgusting.

432. Paul Karp, '"OK to be White": Australian Government Senators Condemn 'Anti-White Racism", *The Guardian,* 15 October 2018, https://www.theguardian.com/australia-news/2018/oct/15/ok-to-be-white-australian-government-senators-condemn-anti-white-racism.

433. Adam Masters, 'Fraser Anning's 'Final Solution' Speech Points to a More Dangerous Threat to Australia', ABC News, 16 August 2018, https://www.abc.net.au/news/2018-08-15/fraser-anning-final-solution-more-dangerous-threat/10123350.

434. Frank Robson, 'By George', SBS, https://www.sbs.com.au/topics/life/feature/george-controversies-australian-government-mp.

435. 'Three Federal Politicians Attended Rally where Antisemitic Speech Given', *Plus 61J Media,* 5 April 2022, https://plus61j.net.au/editors-picks/three-federal-politicians-attended-rally-where-antisemitic-speech-given/.

436. Kristy Campion and Scott Poynting, 'International Nets and National Links: The Global Rise of the Extreme Right – Introduction to Special Issues', *Social Sciences,* 10, No.2: 61 (2020), https://doi.org/10.3390/socsci10020061.

437. Ben Smee, '"Quite Frightening": The Far-Right Fringe of the Election Campaign is Mobilising', *The Guardian,* 4 May 2019, https://www.theguardian.com/australia-news/2019/may/04/quite-frightening-the-far-right-fringe-of-the-election-campaign-is-mobilising.

438. Alex Mann, 'Manifesto Reveals Alt-Right's Plans to Go Mainstream after 'Infiltration' of NSW Young Nationals', ABC Background Briefing, 13 October 2018, https://www.abc.net.au/news/2018-10-13/alt-right-plans-shake-up-of-mainstream-politics-in-australia/10368972.

439. 'Haircuts and Hate: The Rise of Australia's Alt-Right', ABC Background Briefing, 14 October 2018, https://www.abc.net.au/radionational/programs/backgroundbriefing/haircuts-and-hate:-inside-the-rise-of-australias-alt-right/10365948.

440. Mann, 'Manifesto Reveals Alt-Right's Plans to Go Mainstream after 'Infiltration' of NSW Young Nationals'.

441. 'New AFP Taskforce to Protect Federal Politicians and Candidates', AFP Media Release, 20 March 2022, https://www.afp.gov.au/news-media/media-releases/new-afp-taskforce-protect-federal-politicians-and-candidates.

442. Nour Haydar, 'AFP Creates New Task Force ahead of Federal Election to Protect Politicians, Candidates', ABC News, 30 March 2022, https://www.abc.net.au/news/2022-03-30/afp-new-task-force-federal-election-protect-politicians/100952804.

443. Peter Hartcher, 'The Quiet Australians Spoke and They Said 'Enough'', *The Age*, 21 May 2022, https://www.smh.com.au/politics/federal/the-quiet-australians-spoke-and-they-said-enough-20220521-p5anda.html.

444. Mario Peucker, 'A Focus on Violence Creates Blind Spot in Assessing the Far Right Threat', *Fair Observer*, 14 January 2022, https://www.fairobserver.com/politics/extremism/mario-peucker-cve-far-right-violence-terrorism-threat-australia-news-15422/.

445. Ibid.

Lowy Institute Penguin Specials

1. *Beyond the Boom*, John Edwards (2014)
2. *The Adolescent Country*, Peter Hartcher (2014)
3. *Condemned to Crisis*, Ken Ward (2015)
4. *The Embarrassed Colonialist*, Sean Dorney (2016)
5. *Fighting with America*, James Curran (2016)
6. *A Wary Embrace*, Bobo Lo (2017)
7. *Choosing Openness*, Andrew Leigh (2017)
8. *Remaking the Middle East*, Anthony Bubalo (2018)
9. *America vs The West*, Kori Schake (2018)
10. *Xi Jinping: The Backlash*, Richard McGregor (2019)
11. *Our Very Own Brexit*, Sam Roggeveen (2019)
12. *Man of Contradictions*, Ben Bland (2020)
13. *Reconstruction*, John Edwards (2021)
14. *Morrison's Mission*, Paul Kelly (2022)

MORRISON'S MISSION

Paul Kelly

A LOWY INSTITUTE PAPER

When he became Prime Minister in 2018, Scott Morrison was a foreign policy amateur confronted by unprecedented challenges: an assertive Beijing and a looming rivalry between the two biggest economies in world history, the United States and China. Morrison plunged into foreign and security policy by making highly contentious changes that will be felt for decades, not least the historic decision to build nuclear-powered submarines.

Featuring interviews with Morrison and members of his cabinet, this book tells the story of the Prime Minister's foreign policy convictions and calculations, and what drove his attitudes towards China, America and the Indo-Pacific.

PENGUIN SPECIALS

RECONSTRUCTION

John Edwards

A LOWY INSTITUTE PAPER

What kind of future do Australians have?

Until the coronavirus pandemic, nearly two-thirds of Australians had never experienced an economic slump in their working lives. Indeed, nearly half were not yet born when the Australian economy last tipped into recession. Creating a path for Australia through these difficult times requires a careful assessment of where we have come from, where we are, and where we are going.

This Paper, by one of Australia's leading economic voices, examines the fractured state of the global economy and financial system, the ailing US economy and its epic contest with China, the global economic order, and what it all means for us.